MW00423951

THE MYSTERY OF DEATH

ADRIENNE VON SPEYR

THE MYSTERY OF DEATH

TRANSLATED BY GRAHAM HARRISON

IGNATIUS PRESS   SAN FRANCISCO

Title of the German original:
Das Geheimnis des Todes
© 1953 by Johannes Verlag

Cover design by Roxanne Mei Lum
Cover calligraphy by Victoria Hoke Lane

CONTENTS

I

DEATH AS A PUNISHMENT
AND AN END

In creation, God put man in a good world as its possessor and ruler. By means of space God spread out the things subject to man; God created temporal duration, which makes possession possible. But man turned from God and so changed his whole relationship to created reality. God responded by taking back the space originally given: he banished man from paradise. He took back the time originally granted to man and subjected him to pain, toil and death.

Now, when a man awakens to consciousness he finds that things are withdrawn from him; time runs out. If he tries to cleave to God's word, to live a life of faith, he understands that this withdrawal, this separation is imposed as a punishment, but one that man can accept in a spirit of obedience. He can renounce possessions in order to serve God and make atonement, even to the extent of willingly accepting death. Possession and innocence go together, just as the renunciation of possessions goes together with transitoriness, death and existence in the state of original sin. God set the beginning in paradise; walking in paradise, he encountered man in his primal state, in a primal time, a time that was always fresh, never to run out. When a day passed it did not mean that the sum of days remaining was one less. Experience was one day richer, life was not one day poorer. Each day began anew without entailing finitude and transitoriness. The future remained open.

paradise time

When God punishes, finitude enters in: finitude on the part of man and time, tangible at every minute in the finitude of things and in our separation from them. But this finitude contradicts a fundamental longing man has. For man would like to live forever, rule forever, dwell forever in God's sight; he would like to spend his life in peace and unity, in a divinely constituted relationship with God. He would like to do this in the bosom of a divinely created temporal duration. After the Fall, however, men acknowledge that they must come to terms with finite things. Finitude is the mark, not only of their surroundings, but of themselves; it emanates from them. Their sin intervened in God's work; the sentence of finitude lay in their own sin.

Man lives with one eye on death. The fact that he does not know when it will come makes no difference. He cannot live as if this hour does not concern him, as if it does not strike for him, or as if it is so much in God's power (since strike it must) that man can go on living oblivious of it. On the contrary: he must live with a view to this hour; he must keep it in sight, he must let it have the meaning God has given it right from the very beginning: the meaning of punishment. He must evaluate his death in the light of this relationship to God, in the shadow of this relationship to sin. And in everything finite, in every separation he experiences, he must recognize a punishment imposed by God. Not that he should see nothing in his whole existence but sin and punishment; but he must let each thing *be* what, before God, it is intended to be. God banished man from paradise and made him live in a continual awareness of impending death. In God's eyes this situation is for man's good; so man too should accept it as such.

Once the first sin has taken place, death becomes an inner necessity. If God had not instituted death, man could have imagined that, each time he offended God, he could subsequently make it good, supply what he had failed to do, obliterate his turning away from God by turning toward him. He would have felt that guilt and atonement were within his own power, that he could choose a punishment, a penance that would reconcile him with God if he persisted in it long enough. In other words, he would have imagined that he was basically able to redeem himself. But by death and the finite time which leads up to it, God has shown man that his turning away is far more serious than he had thought, so grave that of himself he cannot make it good. God withdraws time from man so that he cannot speculate with it. The destruction of the relationship of repose between God and man gives birth to the *moment,* that is, the uniqueness of a "now" within a time that is running out.

The *moment* comes into existence at the point where the permanent relationship meets its death. Previously there was no irretrievable "now" cutting into temporal duration. There were changes in this duration, but they were full of the promise of future and recurrence. Time was part of man's "possession" that he shared with God—though no precise law could be formulated to express this sharing. God, as Lord, shaped things, but he granted man a share in his shaping activity. Now there is a "here and now" in complete uniqueness. The form of time shows man that he must die, that his existence is proceeding toward a non-existence, an hour over which he has no control. All things with their space and time participate in this withdrawal from him. Things are transitory, the existing conditions can cease to obtain; everything that presents itself (*vorstellt*) to man is also an omen because at the same time it distorts itself (*entstellt*). It changes, distorts, and will eventually disappear. Everything bears the brand of transitoriness and death, and, above all, of guilt.

Previously man did not need to labor in order to preserve his life; now he is compelled to work against the factors of the once-for-all and the transitory. Since the moment passes, he must labor, he must attempt to wrench its transitoriness from it, elicit a fruit from it, impart a kind of permanence to it that will give him a certain residual, human measure of security. It touches him at the level of his bodily existence which is running toward death; to live means to "swim against the tide of death".

Death is the end, and as such it is a mystery. It is not the kind of end which is succeeded by a continuation, a reconstruction. It is simply *The End*, complete cessation. God has totally changed man's relation to his life and environment, but he has not told him what he will do with him when life comes to an end. Yet man has some experience of this end: he experiences the death of his fellow men, he sees them being lowered into the earth, he knows that their bodies decompose, that all human contact with them is broken off. No love, no remembrance is able to call them back. Beyond death, coming into view, as it were, in the gap that death leaves, there is only—God. God, who was before this human being existed, who created and accompanied him, who survives his death, just as he will survive my death and the death of every man and of all generations. And what God will do with his deceased creatures is a mystery.

We can observe how, as man grows, he develops his relationships with his environment, with his fellow man and with God. We can see how each one goes his own way, in faith or in unbelief, blundering into sin or turning away from it. But however men have lived, and whatever they have believed, all of them have died. There are no exceptions. No one has avoided being subject to God's penal law, no one has been able to conjure up the conditions of paradise once more. We cannot put the clock back; we cannot change God's mind about his decision and about the mystery of death. Moreover, man knows that anyone who believes in God turns his soul toward him and in doing so puts all that he does and his entire bodily existence at God's disposal. But when death comes he has to see that this bodily existence succumbs to disintegration; he cannot see what will become of faith and the spirit of faith and obedience. The only visibility God allows him is the visibility of the dead body; what he has in store for the soul he veils in mystery. And the person who wants to come to God in a relationship of faith does not know what God will do with him. The only certainty he has is that this relationship cannot exempt him from the certainty of death and the uncertainty of the hour. He has no knowledge about possibilities his spirit may have to remain in contact with his flesh; nor does he know whether, when his body disintegrates and returns to its constituent elements, the soul will be able to maintain its relationship with God or be sustained in it by God. Both are equally inconceivable to him.

Death creates a very remarkable relationship with one's neighbor. A person can look at the body of a friend and see what, in a very short time, he himself will be, namely, someone who no longer has control of anything; others are in charge of the disposal of his body. In a spirit of friendship and fidelity he can make the arrangements in accordance with the deceased man's requests, if known, concerning the ceremony, the remains and matters of inheritance. But even as he carries out these requests, he becomes aware how incomplete, basically, his knowledge of the dead man was. He realizes how poorly he knows the man's intimate wishes (even if they have often spoken about his impending death) and how he would like to ask him about a thousand tiny details. So, in a most profound way, he experiences how absent his friend has become through death. He may seem to sense a glance from his friend reproaching him for his clumsiness, his lack of knowledge—which now seems like a lack of love.

The most compelling consequence of death is not merely separation but a growing limitation of understanding, the breaking off of a dialogue, a rapport, a love which had thought it was wider and bigger. My friend is dead, but this death tears

holes in my own existence. Not merely in that my
own death comes closer, but more deeply, in that
whole context, things I took to be certain and
understood are now torn down and taken away.
What seemed to be a semirounded totality now
proves to be nothing but fragments. Every death
of an acquaintance and perhaps every contact with
human death—and perhaps even with that dying
that is manifest in the change of the seasons, in the
fading of a flower—confronts man with his own
end, and not as something welcome and familiar
but as a dark and insoluble question. The only
answer he has to it is that death is a punishment
and hence not graspable by the mind; for God
associates punishment most closely with guilt,
which, for man who knows both love and sin,
remains something alien and incomprehensible.
Thus, unavoidably, death and the thought of
death cause man to see his existence as characterized by sin and punishment.

We also notice that the deceased man, who
cherished hopes of many kinds, drew up plans and
commenced projects, has left everything unfinished by his departure. This places a question
mark over all his work, and since the work manifests the intention of the craftsman, the question
mark attaches to him as well. We observe that
death's influence stretches further than we had
thought. Not only does it affect the body, it
spreads over all human planning and reflection.

Even if the project is carried on by others, somewhere or other the hiatus caused by death will be visible. The punishment inherent in death is manifest not only in the dying person but equally clearly in all that surrounded him and was associated with him. Since man's faith relationship with God presupposes a personal relationship between God and man, the mark of death is not merely anonymity (which it would be if it affected man solely as a member of a species); it also puts a personal, once-for-all end to man's personal acts. What he has done cannot be carried on by just anyone. Death is always final. We cannot count up deaths and balance them with an equal number of births. The more personal the contribution made by this individual life, the more it will scatter tokens of death among mankind, tokens which nothing will be able to erase. For punishment is not the same as atonement.

II

DEATH AS DESTINY

In paradise, man lived in open communication with heaven. He did not need to concern himself with his destiny and his future. He lived in temporal duration, unquestioningly, under God's watchful care, which was visible and tangible to him. Heaven was so close that the succession of days did not constitute an opposition to heavenly life. Unknowing, man enjoyed the grace of God. This is simply how existence was, how God had created it. The creature had just come forth from God: the creature's mental world was a world in which God was present. Paradise was not man's creation: it was God's world. And although man was allowed to rule over it, he did not own himself but was at God's disposal. When questions arose, God was there to answer them. But the entire creation had only just come forth from God's creative hand, fresh and new, fully at man's service.

Since sin came into the world, the whole picture has been clouded. Now man has to find his way in a world that is not the world originally intended for him. God's presence has veiled itself from him, and in this darkness one sin begets another.

The mind's world becomes one of sin, the environment becomes an environment of sin, and man becomes isolated in his guilt. And since by nature he is the image of God, he attempts, as far as his powers will allow him, to become equal to God in creation. He, the sinner, creates his own world. He divides up the days as seems best to him. And the things he produces bear the stamp of his own autonomous power. Initially he does this with a bad conscience, feeling that God could call him to account at any minute. But the layers with which he has covered his paradisal nakedness become thicker and thicker; he hides himself further and further away from God and his fellow men; he creates more and more loneliness bearing the mark of his sin. His senses are no longer receptive to God. If God were to walk in his vicinity, as in paradise, he would not be aware of it. He would mistake the Spirit of God for a mere wind. His knowledge is so restricted to himself that God eventually had to send his Son into the world as a man in order to enable men to apprehend him.

To the sinner, death seems to be the end; it seems violent and brutal. Man's plans reach up to the point of death; it does not occur to him to think and plan beyond death. The idea that God has something more in store for his existence, and that therefore he should cultivate an openness to eternity, seems lacking in substance. He cuts his own tiny world out of God's world and adapts his

thinking to this miniature format. All reflection
on what things may have been like prior to sin is
superfluous; the quest for God and the attempt to
steer one's life by him are similarly superfluous.
Whereas in paradise nature was open to the visible
visitations of a supernature, now man creates a
spurious supernature out of the center of his own
nature; he creates a superhumanity out of his human nature. He tries to extend the limits of his
days, the sphere of influence of his power, the
possibilities of his knowledge. He inflates everything in order to satisfy his longing for something
greater, failing to realize that it is only in humility,
in accepting every divinely given limitation, that
it is possible genuinely to encounter the super-
natural. This is the only way to meet God and be
confronted by him, the only way in which heaven
and earth can find each other. Man has dropped
out of his role, lost his endowments and abilities,
and, lest he rush into the arms of God, he runs into
a fiction that has neither reality nor future and thus
is destructive. All he achieves thereby is to extend
the limits of his fears.

Man wants to be his own master within ex-
panding limits. The last limit which he can perhaps push a little further, but not abolish, is death.
He knows from experience what it involves. The
dead man has relinquished his control over life. He
can no longer be included in our accounting. He is
no longer a reality. We who are still alive will not

countenance the idea that his death could be a passing over to God, the decisive expansion. As far as the world is concerned, the dead man is dead. That is the final verdict on him. But in giving this verdict man realizes that he too is mortal; death breaks into his life from the perimeter and settles like mildew over the glamour of the moment. His life becomes one long *angst* in the face of death. He even tries to keep this at bay, looking for ways of escape that will bring peace and contentment in his everyday life and take away the terror that lies in his death and every death.

But where can man conjure up a power strong enough to do battle with what menaces him? And indeed, he is threatened at all points: by sickness, natural catastrophes, unknown enemies, unforeseeable misfortunes that may strike him or any one at any time. Every day he hears of death's latest inroads. So only one thing is left: he must reach beyond death. For the sake of his own peace of mind he summons the dead back. Perhaps the dead have the power he wishes he could attribute to himself. What threatens him must have a cause: it is not to be found in man himself; surely, therefore, it resides in a power somehow related to him, to the world of the living. It must be the power of the dead. Thus arises the idea that the dead have a life of their own. Perhaps they belong to a world where there are neither the wishes nor the desires which make themselves felt in the world of the living; perhaps they take their revenge for all that takes place here contrary to the laws of the realm of death.

In this way man projects the experiences and laws of his existence on to a Beyond he himself has invented. He allows God (who is long dead) to celebrate a pseudoresurrection in human beings who are no longer living. The Beyond is annexed to this world. He uses the realm of the dead to enrich his life. He does this in order to enhance the earthly human being's power over destiny, in order to include in his calculations what eludes all human reckoning. The sinner is bound to calculate. He will not accept that he has lost that power that death has taken from him: he attributes it to the dead. The most he can do, on his deathbed, is to consign his earthly possessions to those who live on. But he cannot bequeath his inner nature, his will to power, to others. He gives it to the dead. And in order to prepare for the hour of his own death, he shows reverence to the dead while he himself is still alive. Thus everything is still referred to himself; this indicates the depth of his forgetfulness of God. He is unwilling to receive his earthly power from the hand of God; accordingly he will not countenance the thought of giving his earthly power back into God's hand when he dies. It would reveal a contradiction that would put a question mark over his whole existence. So, instead, he makes some kind of continuity between this world and the world beyond by attributing to the dead a life patterned after his own earthly life. His cult of the dead is in fact a fear of death, a fear of the ultimate withdrawal of all power from the creature on its return to God.

Maybe, however, the sinner sees nothing in death but the end; with this in mind he enjoys and uses everything available to him, trying to attain a kind of fulfillment and completeness of life on this side of the grave. He manufactures an illusory justification of existence that may satisfy him for as long as he is alive. Once again he invests everything in the service of this fiction; out of his own mind he nourishes his plans for making existence more enjoyable, not doubting for one moment, however, that he is going to his death. He constructs a philosophy of life in the face of the certainty of death. He will enjoy and control what is to hand as long as it is there; death will come soon enough. His attitude to destiny is half resignation, half recalcitrance. On the other hand he is so convinced of the power of his personality that he minimizes the part played by destiny as much as possible. An ego, he wants to rule his own being and nourish it with everything serviceable to it. In this heightening of self, the painful thought of death must be avoided if at all possible.

This game of hide-and-seek will not be difficult in the years when his power is at its full strength; later on he will assume "the wisdom that comes with age" (as he calls it), so that death will not take him completely by surprise. He will take various measures and express certain thoughts about his impending death, giving the impression of a prophetic testament that will prolong his influence beyond death. He professes to regard death as a liberation from earthly limitations. He is not anxious about what comes afterward, choosing to see it as a state of pure nonexistence. This is his armor as he goes to meet his hour, while at the same time he knows that he will *undergo* his own death: it will be something over which *he* no longer has any control.

Death can send heralds in advance when one least expects them. The person concerned is free to refuse to listen to their warning. The objectivity he shows in the face of other people's death and illness fails when his own turn comes. He is always finding new excuses and apologies for the evident signs of his aging and disintegration. As far as death is concerned, he wants to have the last word and tries to make those around him party to it. Thus his dying proceeds in a web of untruth. His death is like his life; he does not want to know anything about an unavoidable encounter with God. He fabricated his life out of lies and now he is

fabricating his death in the same way. Right from
birth, in reality, he was at God's disposal, but he
did not want to know about that, and now he will
not be parted from his not knowing.

The result is that there is not the least connection between the lie he has fabricated and what
will in fact take place. He has a thousand reasons
for not wanting to die: family reasons, business
reasons, personal reasons. They all seem so important that he fails to realize the most obvious
thing. Perhaps he squanders his remaining ener-
gies by fighting against death. It is not a genuine
fight to the death; it takes place at a level of the
mind where the word that attains truth has long
been gagged, although untruth knows that its
time is up. Certainty leaves the field to uncertainty, and the fear that had always been there,
covered up or avoided, can flare up in a vision of
what the truth might be, wrapping the dying
person as in a flame: the fear of what is to come,
the fear of God and his judgment.

The dying man can find nothing in his life that
might be seen as a preparation for this encounter
with the living God. Now he may feel that it
would have been easy, at particular turning points
in his life, to have seized upon some word, reflected on some item of belief, practiced some
attitude that he saw modeled in other people. It
might have represented something of vital impor-

tance to him, too; it might have enabled him to experience his death differently, to retain some hope, to avoid being inundated by *angst*. (It might have enabled him to die in the confidence of the sinner who knows of God's mercy.)

III

DEATH AS PROVIDENCE

When sinful man was driven out of paradise, God
put toil, pain and death as obstacles along his path.
In overcoming them he was to feel his way back to
a right relationship with God. This was not the
same grace as at first, but a favor to be newly won
each time. It was fragile, as he could clearly see
from the fragility of his own existence. Similarly,
the other created things were no longer clearly
oriented to the purposes for which they were
made; in the new order of punishment imposed on
man, they would have to be redirected again and
again to their purposes—by man's strength and
labor. The finitude of things and man's finitude
looked each other in the face. The initial relation
to God, that is, a life of effortless love, could not
be regained. Nor did God keep it always before
man's eyes. Man was not to seek God through the
enjoyment of creation but in the difficulties of a
toilsome everyday existence.

Moreover, the cares and anxieties of life led
unavoidably to death. Each day brought it nearer.
And behind it stood the God whose punishment it
was. Through their disobedience men had torn

away part of God's mystery; his response was to lay upon them the mystery of death, stretching out like a shadow over their lives. Each new turning from God rendered his expression more implacable and harsh. When, at times of reflection, they endeavored to reconcile themselves to God, they were obliged to envisage him as the God of justice, administering the law and punishment; this was the God to whom they turned.

But as for what men might offer God as atonement for their trespasses, it was always an "as-if". They gave him *as-if* gifts, *as-if* sacrifices, since all these things were marked by the vicissitudes of transitory existence and death. This aspect of God's punitive justice could not be erased from even the purest conception of God, the most sincere attempt at worship and obedience. Men could bow to God's power up to the limit where God administered punishment. But they could not give him their death (and hence the entirety of their life) because it was the point where God stretched out his hand to them in punishment. God had put into their hearts a longing for reconciliation; in this longing they could promise sacrifices, but it was always with the tacit condition that they would never have to make them. They were not masters of time.

And so men began to barter and haggle with God. If God would first do this or that, then (and only then) they would give him a thank offering.

They could only thank God for things in the past, for being created and for the benefits he had accorded them so far; the future lay in uncertainty, along with death. And as for death, its uncertain nature made it not merely a distant limit but a constantly threatening and imminent end. They were alive, they were believers, and yet they were like dead men. The closer the idea of death came to them, the more clearly they realized the punishment they had incurred, the more sharply the idea of God came into focus. For God had concealed his presence from them in death, in the actuality of punishment. They had left the God of love and grace behind them; before them was the God of justice. Behind them was paradise, before them the certainty of imminent death. This, for them, was where God's self-revelation was to be found.

Sinful man seeks for God. But since he cannot find him undisguised, in paradisal purity, and on the other hand is unwilling to accept his own condition of total sinfulness as an immutable fact, he tries to find ways of avoiding the truth. He tries to start a dialogue with God from a position of safe concealment, whereas God wants to be close to man, without any hidden secrets or intermediaries. God wants man to experience him in all his uncompromising greatness. That is why he has set man on the path of toil and tribulation, suffering and death; they are there to replace man's attempts at avoidance. Through toil and tribulation, insecurity and limitation, man is to encounter God. A God he cannot dismiss or domesticate or reduce to generalizations. In paradise, man saw God's face clear and defined. The sinner, however, finds it convenient for God's features to be veiled. So God restores the clarity of his countenance through the severity of death and punishment. God wants to be light, not lukewarm. He will no more tolerate vagueness with regard to his own appearance than in man. And when, as a result of sin, the harsh contours of finitude stand out and man chafes against them, it is God's providence that finite man should thus come up against God's infinity. In his limitation he encounters God's eternity; in punishment and death he meets God's judging presence.

It is not as if God were present to man in paradise, whereas now only a shadowy image of him is left. It is a different face of the same God, which, now that man is inhabited by fear, seems more furrowed and more censorious. Man could have dwelt, carefree, in unlimited duration, but he sought diversion in sin and put obstacles along his path to God to keep him at bay. Now God has restricted and blocked the power of those things he originally subordinated to man as objects of his possession. In this way God has to some extent come to meet man: in the event of death (and its consequences and preliminaries), God has, as it were, interrupted his divine infinity and eternity in order to address himself to man. But man does not see this new departure on God's part; he only sees the end. The new beginning remains God's most carefully kept secret. It is as if he regrets having given himself so much to man in the first place, since that resulted in man's thinking he could stretch out his hand to touch God's mystery. Now it is as if God has secured the mystery: the Father has lodged the mystery of the new beginning in the Son; he has given him the power to preserve the mystery of the beginning before the Father's sight, not only during the time of the offer of salvation but for the entire duration of the world, for as long as death exists.

For the present, all this is veiled from man. In spite of the clearly evident nature of the fact of death, death brings man up against a twofold solid wall. Death keeps God from being taken by surprise by man. God remains incomprehensible behind this wall. And even if he could be discovered as God, the mystery would still be hidden in the bosom of his divinity. In a certain sense God is kept out of reach of man's nature and supernature, of his everyday rationality and his faith. And since man's faith operates both on earth and in the presence of God, man too knows that the mystery of death confronts him with a twofold question: What will become of me, human being that I am, when I die? Moreover, what will become of death in the presence of God? What has God in store for me, a single human being? And what, through death, has he in store for the human race?

The question of death can even present itself in youth; but equally it can be delayed until the moment when it becomes critically imminent, when the first unmistakable signs betray its nearness and the human being, with a final effort of mind, endeavors to embrace in a single meaning the course of his past life and what lies before him. Thus the meaning of his death reveals the meaning of his life. Loving life, he does not love death. He clings to his surroundings, to individual human beings, and at all events he loves to exercise his influence among them, his unique doing and being which distinguish him from all others. But however personal he may feel he is, however personal he may like to be, he is aware, nonetheless, that human beings have been created as members of a species. They are all identically begotten and born; they all grow and die. It is only at times when destiny draws unavoidably close that the individual takes an interest in mankind's common lot and becomes aware that it is God's dealing with him, that what threatens him is the Creator's work.

For the most part, the individual sees himself as someone who carries out his occupation in his particular sphere of influence, providing for the needs of family life. He may also regard himself as called to exert influence on a wider stage, to move in wider circles, to do things for which he feels chosen, authorized and gifted. This is a matter of judgment on his part. He is accustomed to use his judgment as a criterion in all issues of the human spirit. He accepts and rejects things depending on whether he finds them congenial or can expect them to influence events. If he is of medium intelligence he will acquire, down the years, a certain skill in judging; he will regard it as satisfactory for most circumstances; accordingly he will act on that basis or else leave things alone. He constructs a world within his environment and fashions it; in it he endeavors to exercise the decisive influence. It is characteristic of this world that it strongly reflects his nature. Even the changes he undergoes, which he himself may not be able to see (and may not wish to see), are reflected in this world, which is adapted to him and is ultimately a fiction. Sooner or later the unexpected will happen, whether it be resistance from outside or illness or accident; it will assert its independence from him, seem to fight against him, and his judgment and the decisions which follow from it will be of no avail. If he is a believer, he will recognize God's voice here, he will see the intervention of Providence, of a power that is stronger than he is, a power with which he must be reconciled and come to some agreement.

The first step in such reconciliation is the realization that there is a higher instance than his own judgment, that there is a Will operating in and with him. (This makes an end of his fictitious world: he must find his bearings in the true world of God,) certain of the promise that those who seek will find. Furthermore he learns this not as an isolated individual but in fellowship with others who are largely unknown to him) Many others have been touched and struck by God in such a way that their world has crumbled and crashed; from its ruins another world, God's world, has slowly arisen. This experience signifies the death of everything that is man's own possession, and above all of his own judgment. It is man's confrontation with a greater judgment, namely, the purposes (however hidden) of God. This encounter, each time it occurs, testifies to God's intervention.

Once man has been inwardly convinced of the fragility of his own judgment, he is really standing in the presence of God. He sees his world collapse around him, this artificial superstructure) he has erected with such toil down the years. (This collapse is the sign that he is ready to listen to God's words) God has brought him to this. God has allowed him to construct this worthless world so that by *this* he may become free for God. His efforts which, from the point of view of his now bankrupt judgment, were futile, were necessary in the plan of the Almighty. He was to be made to see. In the death of what was his own he was to discern the sign of God's life. Suddenly, therefore, it goes through him like lightning: perhaps his own physical death has the same significance! Perhaps what he is now undergoing is the beginning of his liberation. Perhaps it is the shedding of the first layers; and how many more of them, more than he knows, are waiting to be shed, waiting until, in death, God himself strips them away so that his soul, his spirit, all his aspirations become free for God! Death, which revealed its true name, liberation, at the point at which man's world collapsed, will lead his whole being to freedom.

However, this liberation needs to be earned. Life is oriented to it; man's coming face to face with God is the crowning, not of life, but of death. It gives death its full significance. The vision of eternity is its fruit. And yet it would be entirely wrong for the believer to leave it to death to strip away his layers. He must spend the life that has been given him, not according to his own sovereign judgment, but in submitting his own judgment to God's. He must make God's grace the companion of all his moments, so that they all become ripe for eternity. And physical death is only the last liberation of a life that is already surrendered. The vision of eternity is the crowning of a faith, eternal life the crowning of a death merited by a life of obedience. The Creator gives personal being to each of his spiritual creatures so that each one may personally hand over the gift of his existence.

When someone who has never really encountered death before wonders about his life and future, he does so within a particular framework, at least within the immediate context of his being thus-and-not-otherwise. His existence is a closed orbit, and in this sphere he has made himself as comfortable as possible. However he imagines the time before him, he generally envisages it to be longer than the span actually granted him. At a certain point death will draw a strict boundary; for the present he himself has left it open and indistinct. He sees himself relatively unchanged from year to year; he is not aware of anything in himself that would bring about a fundamental change, let alone death. Then, suddenly, someone he loved, someone he met every day, is carried off by death. He feels impoverished, perhaps unjustly injured. His customary routine is upset and he cannot cope with it; he had thought and acted in terms of duration; something in him has an imperious desire for duration. But God uses this death, this utter change, to herald eternity.

When God created time, he did so without in any way affecting the substance of eternity. He did not cut time out of eternity. On the one hand there is transitory time; on the other there is an intact

eternity. And when God visited man in paradise,
when he made himself known through the voices
of the prophets in the Old Covenant, when he sent
his Son and poured out his Spirit, he was revealing
the living relationship between heaven and earth.
Time was always embraced by eternity. And man's
relation to heaven is one of eternity's inalienable
possessions. God has spoken: he waits for man's
response.

Thus the believer knows that the circle of his life
stands on the threshold of the circle of eternity; he
knows that God not merely desires this encounter
but actively brings it about. Of course, the meaning
of creation, of the individual life and of the Church,
is revealed in faith, but its fullness will only come
with and from eternity, to which faith looks.
Through eternity what is transitory acquires a
meaning, and death becomes an element of life,
man's way of going to God. The believer cannot
wait for his physical death to impart this content
to his life; the atmosphere of death permeates the
whole of transitory time and transforms it into a
pre-eternal world.

The death of a loved one casts the person who
witnesses it into profound and lonely grief. If he is
honest, however, he must admit that the hole that
has been torn closes again almost disturbingly
quickly. New tasks, new friends take the place of

the deceased; after a certain period the space for-
merly occupied by him is filled. Were he to return,
one would scarcely know what to do with him.

On the other hand, the one who remains feels a
certain regret that the dead man had to go so soon
without having completed his work. But this regret can be shaken off as sentimentality: life must
go on. If he is a believer, however, he can allow
this death to affect him personally. The dead man
has gone on ahead of him; he has shown him the
way he himself will have to go. How can he
expect his death to be any different? Is it not likely
that he too will have to leave his work unfinished?
Prior to this he hardly ever thought about death,
but now it looms up as something which not only
must be reckoned with: it is something that has
the power to introduce a new order into the existing
situation. It occurs to us that the dead man must
have had similar experiences; what we have gone
through makes us realize that he too must have
experienced such things before his time came. We
may have promised the dying man to look after
and continue his work, his concerns, his hopes,
but it is a promise we can neither give nor fulfill.

No one can do any more than anyone else in the
face of death. This is a shattering thought. Up to
now we had regarded ourselves as people who are
alive, people enjoying the prerogative of life,
allowing the rights of death (our own or that of
others) no proper place in our lives. Up to now

fear-filled orientation

eternal life seemed something secondary, almost something that would only acquire significance in the last moments of life, something to veil and soothe the shudder of the dying man's passing, the fear of judgment and the pain of farewell. Such an attitude does not spring from faith; faith adopts God's proportions. The man with this attitude is governed by fear and refers everything to himself. He takes all of faith's branches, which wanted to grow up into heaven, and bends them down to earth, making the whole dimension of faith earthly and limited. Such a man is acting on earth as if he were still in paradise, as if he could calmly appropriate everything—apart from the apple—to his use. He has reduced his faith to the level of a morality, a norm of decency vis-à-vis his environment. As for everything that might have made him open to God and brought the fulfillment of Christian life through Christ, he has so neglected it that it plays practically no part in his life.

It is high time, therefore, for death to break open this hard shell, to make man aware of God's presence and of the demands of eternal life, which impose burdens on him—the love of neighbor, responsibility for others and for the Church—burdens which always carry a heavenly meaning. Hitherto, this community of action (including that of the Church) was almost a business arrangement as far as he was concerned. He looked for some earthly advantage from it. He liked having a business partner, he liked having his wife's (spiritual) fortune, he liked spending his days in the peace of his home (and conscience), remote from all accusation. But the real community into which death brings us is of a different kind. It is a community that looks toward eternal life. We have been invited to it; we are on our way to it. This one goal and purpose unites us in communion with one another. This is the meaning of our existence, and it is our task, while we are still on earth, to express it appropriately.

IV

DEATH UNDER THE OLD COVENANT

Death is sin's punishment. The story of Abel makes it quite clear that death came into the world through sin. Cain's answer to God's question ("Where is your brother?") is not merely the cynical response of the criminal; it states the general view that, as a result of death, the brother no longer needs "keeping". Even if he *had* been his brother's "keeper" while he was alive, now, at any rate, he was free of him. Such a view is diametrically opposed, not only to the promise of eternal life through the Son, but also to the New Testament commandment of love of neighbor. In the Old Covenant, death involves a terrible aloneness, a forsakenness that is not softened by any further prospect. Death is an end whose terrifying inner dimensions are illuminated by Cain's deed: the man who is doomed to a state of death that has no further prospect is abandoned by his brother and neighbor.

Later on we hear of the great age of the patriarchs. Death seems veiled, as it were, by a fullness of earthly existence. Initially it is simply noted, without commentary. It is always a final conclusion, with one strange exception: Enoch does not die, he is "transported". What becomes of him no one knows. This one rent in the web of death only serves to intensify death's mystery. It weaves a new veil around it, concealing more deeply (while partially revealing) the presence and power of God that stands directly behind it. This "transport" is not that of a vision or the hearing of a divine voice, imparting a mission that is visible among men. It is not something heard that indicates a presence of God, a presence that is confirmed by the task's fulfillment. This "transport" stands in the place of death. Enoch does not return. He is like a first, parabolic halo of grace around the somber mystery of punishment.

Moses, too, does not return from his last ascent of the mountain. He is buried by God in an unknown place. People watch as he disappears in the direction of God. Several times before he had disappeared from sight as he walked toward God, but until now he had always returned, bringing God's words and commands. This time God kept him. He died, but God took care of his death. His death is a mystery, one of a whole series of mysteries that took place in his life, each one confirming the presence of God. Later on again, Elijah is transported, and this time it takes place in front of a witness. The prophet's end is foreknown; someone is there as he disappears from sight. This time the mystery of death is not compressed into the mo-

ment of transport; it does not come like lightning
from heaven. Measures are taken, preparations are
made to broadcast the mystery as widely as possible, extending and exerting its influence in all
directions.

The actual process of Elijah's transporting is
shown in terms of splendor and power that not
only point to God's presence but also present the
Father's world in veiled symbols which engage
man's imagination. We are given a whole dramatic
sequence with a climax at the end that goes beyond
all human expectation; indeed, it even stretches
faith to its limits, making demands that overpower
the sober believer. He is taken further, enabled to
embrace more and greater things. The transporting
of Elijah brings the believing Jew face to face with
a power of God that is far from being exhausted in
the things of this world. It is not enough for this
power to make angels visible and cause voices to
be heard; it can momentarily set forth whole
scenarios of the yonder world, a heightened
reality. God intervenes, from his heavenly life, in
our earthly life. It is not enough for him to confirm the laws of our existence in the way we
expect, to stand as it were behind the system he
has introduced through creation. He does something completely new. He shows us images of
such unexpected richness and truth that we cannot
deny that they are real. What Elisha sees with his
own eyes, far exceeding all powers of imagina-

tion, is no dream. He picks up the cloak of the departing prophet and works miracles with it.

In addition to this, the prophets announce things which, while they remain very mysterious, can show us a greater fullness of faith and explode the limits of existing reality and of those things we have grasped in some fashion. It becomes more and more clear that God inhabits a heaven that is uninterruptedly concerned for the earth, a time-lessness that is so alive that our temporal reality pales in comparison, a fullness that causes our life to seem poor and scant of significance. But when God acts in this way, when he apparently suspends the laws he has implanted in our existence, he manifests his will to give a new dimension to our life, not only through the words of prophecy but also through his own inherent reality. One feels justified in linking the voices from above, the visions of heaven and the transporting of Enoch and Elijah: they are pieces of a whole that is as yet invisible.

Not-having-died is not a mere negative. It is something positive of infinite importance: it implies that there is room for man in God's world. The world into which Enoch is transported and the power to which Elijah is summoned to yield himself remain unknown. But this unknown world is the same one which revealed itself from heaven to the prophets. Indeed, in Elijah the two coincide, for the prophet knows of his coming disappearance and is concerned to leave an account of it behind him. But his words, in spite of their prophetic character, are overtaken by God's reality. It is a great thing for a man to possess some insight which is fulfilled in God; but it is even greater when God intervenes to imbue this insight with the power of bringing about his own manifestation.

This implied a huge incursion on God's part into the closed world of men. It was a world that was closed since sin entered in. For the sinner (and the same was true for the man of the Old Covenant), God's world, heaven, seemed something utterly beyond, like the planet Mars seems to us. God's planet was ruled in its own way along the lines indicated by the laws of God; as such it claimed man's respect. There was hardly any question of a personal relationship with it. Death seemed to be the end of human reality, evincing an even greater contrast with the divine world. And as for the signs which God gave to men in visions, they were so rare as to have insufficient effect on their way of looking at things.

Now, however, came the prophecies announcing the coming of the messiah from God. This time heaven itself was in motion; the divine life was setting out on its way toward human life. Once again faith was stretched in a new way by an event that could only be envisaged as God's perfect miracle over and against the laws governing the world. A miracle over life and death, a complete

transformation, which the men of the Old Testament glimpsed in the prophecies. It gradually
became part and parcel of their faith and hope,
although its substance was beyond their grasp. At
last there seemed to be the promise of an end to
their exile; their relationship with God seemed to
have been overtaken by a superior power, a
superior relationship instituted by God himself.
This relationship was of such dimensions that, if it
were eventually to be implemented, it would burst
upon the world like a catastrophe. Natural events
like wars or storms became images of what was to
come, and God himself gave signs, such as the
burning bush, the pillar of fire or prophetic words
or visions, to create confusion in man's pseudo-
order.

Thus man was kept in suspense, aware that the
world he had built for himself in sin could not
elude God's grasp and would eventually have to
face final collapse. His life was lived with a view to
this event. And the event that promised to link
heaven and earth in a new way would not come to
a halt in the face of the event of death. Man came
to understand that what he considered to be final,
God could transform and revalue. Not only did
the concept of God's righteousness infinitely surpass the idea of human justice, it left room for
many things that could not be put into any concept
whatever.

So, gradually, even the dead and their fate were drawn into the great unrest and expectation. Death was no longer purely and simply the end: now it meant being handed over to an uncertain destiny in which God, through his promises, occupied a place. God made a place for himself; man did not make it for him. God contradicted the closed world of the sinner by the might of his action. God's word was the absolute here-and-now that could intervene at any moment in the world, in human life, even beyond death.

In response to this word there arose a hope (although no one could grasp its substance) that even embraced the dead. The prophets' word that the believer encountered was pregnant with meaning, not so much with things to be understood as with a mysterious presence of divine life. It was a word that summoned men to listen, but it also addressed senses that were higher and more alert, a receptivity that had to come from God's world and which man only inadequately possessed. But even this muffled hearing was sufficient to make man look forward to a time when he would listen with full acuity and to matters of ultimate significance. Each prophetic word seemed to contain the inchoate presence of a full and complete Word. Listening to it, man conquered his fear of death. Turning away from it, he sank into death's absoluteness. But this word was so powerful that it embraced all that was beyond man's grasp, which thus lost its menacing and troubling aspect, and transposed man into a state of pure hope. The believer was like a person who takes nourishment without realizing how much energy he will acquire thereby.

V

DEATH AS GOD'S ACTION

Man constructs a concept of his life, partly out of the events that take place in his environment and partly from what he can make of them or would like to make of them. (Objective elements are yes! entangled with subjective ones,) and man often finds it hard to separate the given from what he has added to it. If he has a conventional belief in God and does not accord it any power to transform his existence, while he will pack this concept of God among his life's baggage, it will be a hindrance to him rather than a help. The concept will tend to shrink and be ultimately reduced to a few common garden variety moral precepts. However, if the believer's God is the living God, his life will be continually remodeled by his faith; its determining values will be continually revalued. Things have meaning only to the extent that they lead to God, come from him and can be placed at his service. We cannot play with God as we can with a concept that has only as much importance as we allow it to have; God is so much the living God that the believer has no choice but to consign himself entirely to God's guidance and let him take responsibility. Where man himself has to take responsibility, he does so in the sight of God, entrusting the ultimate fulfillment to him. And this means putting one's whole reliance on God's word, being nothing but a response to this word.

Such a man lives before God in a peace that is like a return to the early days of creation; he experiences God's presence and nearness. However, this man knows something that Adam did not know, namely, that not only his life, but his death too acquires meaning in God. All meaning resides in God. Without him everything would be literally meaningless, that is, not merely contradictory or nonsensical but prefixed by a minus sign; its privative character would be noticeable at every turn. But if a person seriously tries to locate all meaning in God, while he will become far more aware of his own limitations, he will continually be meeting realities unfamiliar to ordinary life, things that have their life in God and cannot be reached by reasoning but only by prayer. Such things are disclosed in the dialogue between God and man, when God utters his word and man endeavors to be nothing but a response to it. Thus prayer opens up a realm of superlife, of divine vitality. Outside prayer, however, its substance must appear completely unreal, nothing but soap bubbles and utopian notions. To be grasped as reality, genuine faith must yield genuine prayer, and God himself must infuse his meaning into the word of prayer; he must accompany the thoughts he inspires so that they are filled solely by that which is his.

Once the meaning of human life has become so boundless, constantly brimming over into God, man realizes that his death cannot be an exception to this law. What comes alive in prayer is so great because it belongs to God's eternal life which bursts the confines of our earthly life. God has not created us for time, but for his eternity. What is eternal is prior; the divine is what has substance and permanence, and the intimations we have of the life of God in our temporal life are a guarantee that we have been called to a life that is eternal.

God does not play with us as with little children, showing us things and then hiding them. When he shows us things, he does it to spur us on, to put leaven into our lives, to hold out a promise that goes beyond all time and is something of his eternity. God's greater nearness, making us feel the absoluteness of his eternal presence, does not create an abyss between him and us; it does not remove him to inaccessible regions. Thus we can see that the tiny measure of eternal life we manage to grasp here and now comes from him and is revealed in our earthly life (and this includes death) by a special grace. In this light, our life and death seem an episode on the way to eternal life. Thus, the more convinced we are of God's eternal life, the more we bear it within us. The relationship between this life and eternal life shifts, within us, in favor of an increasing preponderance of eternity. This life retains meaning only in the light of the eternal. As for us, we are already children of eternal life even while we are still on earth.

If man's true life lies in this prayer dialogue with God, we must see death as the moment when God's word falls silent, when the word is no longer or not yet audible. We could understand the connection between the Old Covenant and death in this way: the whole Old Covenant is again and again characterized by a failure to hear the voice of God; this is its ultimate conclusion. The New Covenant, by contrast, is the complete reinstitution of the divine Word. As the new Adam, the incarnate Son will render the word audible in a fresh, clearer, more direct and all-embracing way. It is as if man has failed to hear the Father's voice, and the Father, in agreement with the Son and the Spirit, has found a new voice to bear witness to his life. Or as if the Father's voice had hitherto masked the voice of Son and Spirit (in the inner-trinitarian dialogue), whereas now, at the creation of the New Covenant, the fullness of the divine word resounds, a triune word of grace that ultimately drowns out all that is human. Seen in this way, death is a waiting for the Son's voice; it is the soul's waiting in a state of suspense until, in the Son's compassion, the Father calls to it and takes possession of it.

The anxiety associated with this suspense is the punishment for man's sin. Now death appears to be God's way of forcibly putting man at his disposal, for the dead man cannot do anything for himself and knows that in his absence, as it were, others will act in his regard and he will simply have to let them. His absence means that he cannot act in the present. But this letting-things-happen is not the same as when the believer in prayer lets things happen, surrendering himself to God and desiring God to fashion him according to his design. It lacks two elements: the praying person wants to be transformed, whereas the dead man's time for wanting things has passed. The one who prays can collaborate by his own self-surrender; the dead are denied all possibility of collaboration. When the person who prays asks that things may take place according to God's will, he does so with some knowledge of what God may require of him; ultimately everything always comes down to service. The dead man has nothing to look forward to but judgment, and a judgment that is alien and unknown to him. Where service is concerned, the person who prays has a certain norm to which he can refer, but with regard to judgment there is no measuring rod. In judgment he is obliged to submit to something immeasurable, which is nothing other than *God's* measure.

What strikes us most about the visible appearance of a dead person is the fixed expression, his noninvolvement and the total lack of contact. The bystanders' words, concepts, cries of grief or help are no longer of any use to him. As far as the living are concerned, the dead man exists in the mode of absence. The only way of communicating with the dead is through prayer; our concerns, requests, wishes, our endeavors to help the deceased person must be addressed entirely to God; we must seek assistance from God's level. Instead of doing things ourselves, we have to ask for God's help. And if this is how things stand for us who are alive—that we are unable to achieve anything on our own— how much more is this true for the dead? The dead man has been utterly relieved and stripped, as it were, of his own self, so that he may participate in that which is God's. He no longer has any choice, any overview (no more than the person who prays for him); he is under external compulsion. He has been violently torn away from the earth and brought into a world of judgment, a world resounding with the voice of God, a world governed by prayer in a way that was hitherto unknown to him. And this new world is not opened up to him through his own efforts but by death.

The sight of the dead man is an admonition to the living. Not merely because it reminds him of the salvation of his soul, and that he should use the passing days to more effect, perhaps turn over a new leaf morally, start something new and abandon something old. Rather, this sight should cause him to recognize that reality of the yonder world which is the only reality as far as the dead man is concerned. It should become a new reality for him too, in life, perceived by his earthly senses in a way that God has made possible to faith. So death opens up a new way of faith and brings one of heaven's realities to earth. It expands the sphere of God's action. Death is not a punishment to be absolved within a certain period of time: it is a voice speaking from within life, unknown eternity operating within transitory time. At the most profound level it is a word from God, part of his teaching.

This teaching attains its fullness in the appearance of the Son, who undergoes the death of all and, through the Father's power working in him, implants the resurrection at the very heart of this death. There is no way resurrection can take place except through death. For faith, his return to the Father as one who has been raised from the dead becomes the sole source of our participation in eternal life. The resurrection is the goal of redemption. It *is* redemption. Human nature is not redeemed for temporal life, but for the risen life of the Son. The signs of death that cling to human nature become heralds of the resurrection. All that separates man, inevitably, from his temporal existence constitutes his path to heaven. Suffering of every kind, toil, the process of aging, the community of sinners—all are transformed under the sign of the Son's resurrection into invitations to eternal life, pledges of Christ's presence in each one. And Christ is not an idea: he is the Risen One who adopts his brothers into his resurrection.

The resurrection is one of the Father's secrets. Looking at the two kingdoms of creation, heaven and earth, which both belong to the Father, the believer realizes that the Father's kingdom in heaven has always remained in accordance with the Father's will and purpose, whereas the earth has changed because of man's sin. (Comparing the eternal and the transitory realms, we are bound to decide in favor of heaven.) We see the Father's intervention on earth, the permanence of the Church, man's faith and striving; we see conversions, experience miracles (or hear of them), learn how the eternal world breaks through into the transitory. Not until we are confronted with the resurrection, however, do we know that heaven's victory over earth is total. Only then do we realize that the Father can change even the last enemy, death, into eternal life, punishment into the highest reward, fear into eternal bliss. (The resurrection of the sinner is God's most extreme, most extravagant way of dealing with man. It is not merely a victory; it is a radical reversal of everything we have heard of, experienced and expected.)

Now it almost seems as if death has been invented in order to give man ultimate proof of God's superior power. This ultimate proof, however, is not to be found finally in death, as experienced by human beings; it is continually present in the life of faith. It is not I who live, but Christ who lives in me: this is the proof that God's power is almighty even in this world. It is not that the believer has the power of living the life of someone else: it is God who has the power to pull the life of faith through the restrictions of the transitory so that it may share in the life of the Risen Son. This is no symbol or parable: it is reality, a reality that comes from God and lays hold of man, even when the latter's understanding fails. It fails because the distance between God and man is not obliterated; man *can* (not must) remain a sinner. And most of all it fails because he is immediately overpowered by the greatness of what is happening to him. The Son has set before him his life's goal: the Father's perfection; but he also gives him the way to attain it, namely, his own, perfect, filial being, as a presence within him. Of course the Son is the only one who can live on earth as perfectly as the Father in heaven. But in his perfection he gives himself to the believer, so that "I live, yet not I, but Christ lives in me", Christ, who lives in the perfection of the Father.

The sinner who also has faith recognizes death's signature on his transitory life; but he also recognizes the signature of the Risen Lord who is resurrected for him. His death, making visible his decline and collapse, has already been overcome by the Risen One. He no longer needs to stare at himself and count his weaknesses, despairing of his inadequacy: he can look at the heavenly Lord who lives within him—whose earthly influence is visible only to faith, not necessarily in terms of experience—or he may ponder the Lord's earthly path and be overwhelmed by this victory on the part of eternal life. (This does not mean that his human death will be any easier because of it,) nor that he will not have to undergo days, weeks or months of struggling. But he will be certain of surviving the struggle and death itself. Whatever his death may look like from the perspective of this temporal world, he is on his way to God's victory. All the obscurity of dying is absorbed into the preeminent clarity of eternal life.

VI

DEATH, WHERE IS THY STING?

Death will retain its penal aspect until the end of the world. In death's mirror man recognizes how perverse and sinful he is. But in this whole dimension of punishment, he should also see the Father's solicitous care for man. The same Father who, as Creator and Lord of the Old Covenant, appointed death, also permits death under the New Covenant. God does not surrender his rights as Creator and Owner; this explains all the measures he takes in dealing with man. The sting of death is that it is a punishment. But just as our being sinners is transformed by the Son's coming, so death's penal aspect is also transformed. From the moment the Son surrenders himself for us, not only humanity as a whole, but each individual with his whole destiny and death is personally contained in the Son's sacrifice.

The Son did not come to put an end to the Father's work, to the measures he has taken, but to show them to be based on the love of the Trinity. When, as a final sacrifice to the Father, he gives his life for sinners and dies the death of the cross, it is quite natural for him to love this sacrifice, to love his own death, since it expresses the love in which he makes himself an offering to the Father. He loves the work he performs on the cross because it is to bring the world back to the Father. This cross is the last achievement of his so-inventive love, its highest achievement. And even though it is bought at the price of the greatest suffering, there remains that unity between death and resurrection, between love for the Father and love for men, between the joy of the incarnation and the bitterness of dying.

So we are presented with a twofold contemplation of death: we see ourselves dying as sinners, punished by death for our sins; but at the same time we are privileged to know that our death is kept safe in the Son's death, that it shares in the work effected by the Son's death, and that therefore, together with him, it is going to meet the resurrection. Thus its bitterness becomes blessedness. Yet the bitter side is not simply identical with the blissful side; the two are not confused. There remain two ways of looking at this, corresponding to two experiences which every human being has to undergo in some way or other. For even when a believer is dying the most painful death, receiving no consolation in the midst of his dying, he cannot say that faith never consoled him in any way. And as for the person undergoing an easy death, perhaps not even aware of it, he cannot say that he never had any misgivings at the idea of having finally to leave this life. What the Son achieves through death rests on the foundation of what the Father has done; it neither cancels it out nor coincides with it. The bitterness of the punishment can be both contemplated and experienced separately from the joy of the resurrection. The Son did not come to give us a life of faith that is proof against all difficulties and doubts, a kind of oblivious happiness removed from everything that is hard and painful. Such a life would not be a following of Christ.

All Christian sacraments wear this twofold aspect of death; they cannot be put into the straitjacket of a one-sided truth. They are so much the expression of the Son's life, as he lived it, that they contain both elements: his sacrifice and the joy in which he makes it. This goes right through everything, even to the requiem: the mourners, who as yet hardly realize the full extent of their loss, know all the same that the deceased rests in God's hands, sharing the destiny of the children of God, no longer subject to the vicissitudes of this world. And if we were to try to incorporate Saint Paul's vision of death into our faith, we would come across the same twofold aspect: according to Paul, death is like a battle between the mortal and heaven; its outcome is the victory of heaven, and the battle itself exhibits various successive phases that are indecisive, because man himself is invited to join in the struggle concerning his own death.

In other words, man must collect "merits" with a view to his death. It is not simply a case of doing good in order to please God; rather—and this is the Pauline aspect—he is to appear before God as a faithful soldier, bringing him both the work of grace (the Lord's resurrection) and the work of the sinner who has fought his way through to God (and suffers death as a punishment). Ultimately, furthermore, this is the only way man can face himself. The Christian should not be surprised by death nor even by the thought of death, for his whole life is a diligent preparation for death. All that he does in this regard rests on grace, for the Christian could not fight unless Christ, the Risen One, were living in him. It is the Lord's death that helps him die his Christian death; indeed, it so incorporates him into the Lord's dying that the Christian can suffer "what is lacking in Christ's afflictions".

The sting of death is sin; as long as there are sinners the relationship between sin and punishment will remain. But we must also say, "as long as God stands over against sinners". For in this case, punishment is a preliminary stage leading to sanctification through the Lord's death. The death of each individual sinner has to point to the Lord's death and is vanquished in it. The mystery of the communion of saints in the Church has a parallel in this communion in the Lord of the deaths of all sinners. In reality no one dies his own death, for the death he is to die is swallowed up in the Lord's death. Furthermore, through the cooperation of Father, Son and Spirit, the Church has a role in the administration of death, just as she has in the administration of prayer. The man who knows he himself is kept safe in the Lord and in the Lord's cross and death, sharing in his resurrection, also knows that every one is his brother, present with him in the same Lord. There is no confusion in the Lord, but a lively interaction whereby the Lord, who dies for us all, can give each individual the very death the Church needs at this particular time.

So, if we endeavor to live for the Church, we can be sure that we will be privileged to die for her too. Not in the sense of some heroic deed, not that we shall have a total picture of the task laid upon us, not through being mistaken for someone else nor as a result of our own arbitrary choosing: our dying for the Church will be part of our being chosen, part of our self-surrender for the sake of service, which may attain that fulfillment in death which was denied to it in life. This means that we cannot attempt by empirical means to extract the sting of death, that is, the effect of sin in death, from our own death. Certainly we can say, "The

Lord has died for *me*; he has absolved *me* from my sins through the sacrament of penance." But he has also done the same for others, and our faith's ultimate task is to renounce not only every exclusiveness but all personal prerogatives whatsoever. Just as a religious puts his fruitfulness at the Church's disposal and a nun may have to be a mother to countless orphans, we too can entrust what is ultimate and most personal to us, the significance our death may have for humanity, to the anonymity of service in the Church. This is how we give our death for the Church.

In the Lord's earthly life, all his fruitfulness is summoned up at the cross with a view to his death; since his incarnation signifies fellowship with us, we too, within the Church and together with him, may gather up our Christian willing and hoping with a view to his cross. In personal terms this means that our death, whatever form it may take, is to be seen as the final concentration of our surrender to God. Just as religious, as part of their self-surrender, try to renounce controlling their own work and setting their own goals, we too can do something similar with regard to our death, dying not *our* death but the death given us by the Lord through the Church. In this way the sting of death—that is, death as experienced—can be compared to the sting of work: ultimately it is no concern of ours, for in Christian terms it is one

of God's mysteries that our death has the particular
face he gives it, just as, if we have chosen to follow
the Lord, our life's work has the particular face
God gives it. Renouncing a personal death, a death
we have envisaged and manipulated, is only the
counterpart of renouncing a life we ourselves have
fashioned.

VII

I AM THE RESURRECTION
AND THE LIFE

The Son of God utters this word in the midst of his life. He does not say, "I am alive". He distinguishes himself from every other life. He claims that he himself is life; he does not *participate* in human life: he says he *is* life, whole and entire; more than that, he is the resurrection, too. This is something that hardly has any meaning within human experience. We are familiar with the individual's life and death, but here the Son is saying that he is all life, man's life and God's life. It is as if he permeates all life in order to gather it into himself, as if there is no life outside his, as if we are to understand that every-thing that is alive in us is created by the Father, comes from him and should be grasped as the here-and-now voice of God. It is made audible to us in a new sense, gathered into one by the Son to be newly bestowed each time.

When the living Father created the world, he put life into it. He created it from nothing. He took the lump of earth in his hand and breathed life into it. We can imagine this process being repeated countless times: God is continually creating new life, placing it beside what is already there. It is different each time, and yet it is something brought forth and bestowed by him, something destined—through sin—for transience and death.

But in this word of his, the Son leaps over death. He is life, he is the resurrection. For the present, whatever comes after life and before the resurrection has no meaning at all. The two things, life and resurrection, are in close conjunction; they form an indivisible unity, so much so that neither can be understood without the other. The Son's life does not make sense apart from the resurrection, nor does the resurrection make sense apart from his life. These words are the background against which he will raise Lazarus from the dead, after having spoken aloud with the Father. What he performs is a divine work, carried out by him who became man; it is a work that is expounded by his words. He is life; but he is also that resurrection that is brought about by God. And since each is necessary to explain the other, this means that his life is inwardly informed by the resurrection principle, that is, the relationship to that divine reality, that higher world to which his prayer journeyed. Since he gives his life to all, since his life pulsates in all who live, he also imparts his resurrection in the same way. It is a kind of osmosis.

Thus the individual's life has become a life that is being raised from the dead; for him too life and resurrection (if it makes any sense to speak of these

things in the context of an isolated individual)
have become an indivisible unity. (The miracle of
the Eucharist can help us to understand this) by
means of it, the Son's life enters each individual
believer. It has the effect of making us live no
longer for ourselves: he lives in us. Now, however, everything is even more condensed: he does
not need first to give us his life in the sacrament in
order to impart his life to ours; he *is* life, right
from the outset. Note, however, that he says this
when death is close. Every believer knows, from
personally sensing the approach of death or from
experiencing the fear of death, that life never
seems so worth living as when it is threatened by
death. He knows that he can only bear the thought
of death because the thought of resurrection is
stronger.

The Lord knows that this is how we are; he
knows our fear. And he takes the opportunity
presented by this moment just before working the
miracle, to direct attention to *his* life, to the resurrection which *he* is. It is as if Martha is especially
open, in this moment of grief and fear, for the new
idea of life. At the same time the Lord wishes to
use his friend's death, which augurs his own—it is
the chalice that he must drink—to show what he is
in his hidden being. "Do you believe this?" he
asks Martha, bringing her into a new faith relationship with him. She must utter her Yes in
reply, and then her life will be poured forth into

the Lord's life. I am the resurrection: every anxiety we have, every attempt we make, every calculation —all is taken up into him and dissolved. I am the life: there is no room any more for fear or anxiety. This transfer takes place in faith. For the present, death's role withdraws to the background.

Lazarus in his tomb only provides the occasion for this handing over of faith, this being adopted by the Lord. Death is the soft background music, an opportunity used by the Lord to reveal himself as he is. He is life, but this life is not defined by being compared to human death; it is eternal life, shared with the Father, and resurrection is the return to the origin of this life. In fact, it is a connection between the eternity that has been and the eternity that is to come; it is the bridging of both in a single life so that the Son's life on earth is no different from his life in heaven, his life in time is inseparable from his life in eternity. Ultimately every life, even the sinner's, is taken up into the Lord's perfect life in such a way that it is transformed in him and becomes the life of grace. Resurrection is not only the hyphen linking eternity before and after earthly life; it also means that the Son retrieves the sinner's life; he explodes all human life and incorporates it into his own.

The Son is both life and resurrection. This means that his life is unthinkable apart from heaven. It means that he became man not only in order ultimately to raise men up with him; equally, it was to reveal a divine life in the very midst of mortality and finally, having completed his mission and returned to heaven, to imbue men with resurrection life as a demonstration of his truth. This word is spoken not only to Martha, it is addressed to all believers. But since the Son's love for all men cannot be separated from his love for the Father and the Spirit, this human word uttered by the Son is also addressed to heaven. Thus it is as if, between himself and the Father, the Son wishes to minimize the importance of his own death, to assure the Father that he, the Son, feels himself to be entirely the ambassador of his eternal life; to give the Father new confidence, so to speak, with regard to the coming passion.

Now, when the Son asks the Father to raise up Lazarus, he covertly includes himself in his request. He does not want to be the one taking action, he wants to allow the action to take place; he wants what is to happen to him to happen to Lazarus. But while the Father acts upon Lazarus, in response to the Son's call, in the once-for-all dimension of temporality, he is also the One who is addressed by the Son from all eternity, who eternally gives him life. And the resurrection which the Father will work in his body is as certain as that he, the Son, is life, as certain as the raising of Lazarus that is taking place before the Son's eyes. Finally, then, it is a word of victory, uttered for the sake of believers and in order to give the miracle its

fullness and ultimate meaning. It is also addressed
to the Father, once more reiterating the Son's Yes
to his mission.

Lazarus' dead body is a kind of bodily proof,
presented to men and to the triune God, of the
objectivity of death. It is surrounded by the subjective grief of the sisters, which is also objective
in so far as the sisters consider their brother's death
to be final. The Lord also weeps and shudders. He
weeps for the earthly loss of a human friend; he
himself is so human that he is affected by the
human mourning around him, mourning the
death of a friend and sharing the grief of those he
loves. The situation is completely human, and
now the divine dimension enters it in a twofold
manner. First in the form of the miracle itself, and
then in the form of the Son's resurrection which
stands behind the raising of Lazarus. In this latter
case there is an exchange of places: the Son hands
over his very self into the being of Lazarus, and
Lazarus' being is taken up into that of the Son, so
that the Father can perform the raising of Lazarus
in the Son who is the resurrection. This is a proof
of the Son's effective influence on earth, a fruit of
Christian teaching. First he hands the miracle over
to the Father: he must perform it. But because the
Father is just as alive in him as he is in the Father,
the Son, having called upon the Father, takes over
the function of representing the Father on earth.
He is the one through whom the Father does his

Will on earth, the Son who allows the Father's Will to operate in him.

Here we have a whole interplay of persons and situations. In heaven there is the Father, who is called upon by God the Son, who as man needs to allow the Father to work, and who both as God and as man possesses full assurance that his petitions are heard. Then there are the mourners, who are also moved by hope, and finally the dead man. But neither the sisters nor Lazarus are conceivable in this situation apart from the Lord's presence. (The faith which the Lord has given to the sisters lives in them as his life.) In the case of the dead Lazarus, we cannot speak of a presence of the Lord, in faith, in the same way, but we can speak of that presence in virtue of which the Son can say of himself, "I am the resurrection and the life". Thus love flows around in a circle: from the Father to the Son and on to the believer. Initially Lazarus appears as the object of this whole love. He himself can no longer love since he is dead; all he can do is passively receive love, he cannot perform it actively. But (the Lord's love is so strong that his presence even becomes visible in the dead man in the form of resurrection and life.) It is so strong that the Lord who is resurrection and life, in commanding Lazarus to rise, produces a proof of who and what he is: Lazarus rises in obedience from the dead to confirm the Lord's words and complete the circle of love.

Prior to this, it seemed that the cords of living love led to Lazarus and ended there. But now they extend beyond him: he was so loved by the Son that now he is the one whom the Son raised, demonstrating the truth of the Son's word, risen not merely to a life which the Creator has restored to him for a further space, but to life that is new, given to him out of the Lord's love. In this way Lazarus becomes a proof of the necessity of the Lord's incarnation, a miracle ratifying the testimony of the Word and demonstrating that the Son is present not only in the living but also in the dead. Lazarus becomes a demonstration of the Lord's miracle-working love.

The death which is overcome in Lazarus' case is full of significance in anticipation of the resurrection. Lazarus' dying, in so far as it prefigures the Lord's dying, serves to illustrate the power of the resurrection. It is a case of showing what God can and will do, both as Creator and as Redeemer. The Father, summoned by the Son, perfects the work of his creation; but he does so by affirming the Son and manifesting his unconditional, miracle-working love, a love which carries out the words it utters. Thus his words "I am the resurrection and the life" acquire a new meaning. He is life in himself, complete, visible, just as he is seen by those around him. But this life which he *is* is a life of participation, communication, of giving and self-giving, a life that will allow no death in his presence. And [this life is love, but the act of surrender is fulfilled in suffering] For the duration of this suffering, everything the Son is—life and resurrection—is placed so entirely in the Father's hands that, from the outside, nothing is visible but death. (In this sacrifice the Son has emptied himself not only of his being, but also of his meaning) For the meaning of his mission was to be life and resurrection, to bring them, to lay them in the Father's hands.

On the cross, when both the Son's mission and the Father are invisible, life and resurrection remain with the Father. He has taken back the Spirit of the Son, and so it seems as if he has nothing more to do with this dying man hanging on a cross. The Father has the Son's being with him; this is how he is able to survive this hour, whereas the Crucified One dies completely abandoned. In his hands the Father holds not only the proofs but also the matter of those proofs, namely, the Spirit of the Son who said, "I am the resurrection and the life". The Crucified ends his life turned toward the men because of whom he is dying, in order to redeem them; but he is also turned toward the Father and the Spirit, knowing that he has given everything back. And as for his being the resurrection and the life, he has given that back too. He is once more at the disposal of the Father who sent him.

But the Son, who dies on the cross, is a divine Person, from whom the Spirit proceeds as he does from the Father. And now, the Spirit having been breathed back from the cross to the Father, (the Trinity-in-Unity acquires a face that we can call the resurrection face) The Son surrenders his Spirit, and as he does so the Father reaffirms the Son's being. In so far as the Son is God, together with Father and Spirit, this affirmation is a matter of course. But he also breathes out his human spirit, and it is inseparable from the Spirit of the Church.) He, the Incarnate One, is the Bridegroom who does not leave his Bride when he returns to heaven. He presents her to the Father; at his resurrection she will appear together with him, and he anticipates this by sending back his Spirit. The Father will recognize in him the Spirit of the Son, but under the form of the Spirit of the Cross, where the Son has bestowed his Spirit on the Church.

At this point, however, all things go out into the mystery of eternity. As for the idea of the Son's handing himself back on the cross, we can only follow it for a certain distance, then it breaks off; for of course the Son, in returning his being— and he is the resurrection and the life—to the Father and dying on the cross, does not cease being God) All the same, in this fragment of understanding we can discern one of the many meanings of the cross: the recognition of the Church by the Father in heaven. But the Father remains the infinite God, giving us an idea of the same infinity in the Son and the Spirit. (On the cross, to all appearances, the Son has become nothing but a finite point; from the perspective of his visible place in the world he seems to act as a separate and finite person vis-à-vis the Father. But the Three-Person God has never ceased being One and Infinite.) Incarnation and cross are a way of looking—from a finite vantage point—into God's eternal being. (Here, where the completed mission is given back to heaven, it becomes immeasurable, since it is commensurate with God) (All that has been revealed returns back to unity, thence to renew its influence and fruitfulness) And where finite contours seem to appear in order to facilitate our human grasp, (everything immediately refers back to God's unity) In this process of handing back, man's faith is also taken up into heaven; the Church is taken up into heaven. This is what resurrection means. From all eternity, resurrection is indivisible, eternal life in God.

VIII

DEATH AND THE CHURCH

The Son has instituted the Church; she is his Bride. But she is made up of human beings, and he must entrust her administration to human beings. Nor are these two aspects foreign to each other, for the Church is a living unity. The Church is what the Lord intended and fashioned, filled with and strengthened by the Spirit at Pentecost. She possesses the sacraments and administers the Lord's inheritance, constantly encountering the eternal Bridegroom in a supertemporal freshness and youth. And those who form the Church are the saints—which means believers—and together they constitute the communion of saints. They are genuine human beings, placed in the Lord's presence not only as a community but also most definitely as individuals. They were created as individuals by the Father, given genuine responsibility; it is a responsibility they share with and for all others, but, for that very reason, it is a personal one. These individual human beings die. They die the death which sin has brought into the world and which is bound up with fear and uncertainty. But, since they are Christians, they also die the death which the Lord has died for them. In their most personal dying, therefore, they are drawn into the Lord's dying for our sins.

On the cross, the Son of Man underwent extreme anguish and utter abandonment. Both in his life and in his death, the Christian can only share in the Son's personal anguish because it has been suffered, perfectly and once-for-all, by the Son. In addition he dies his own death; but he does so in faith, in the communion of the saints, that is, surrounded, tended and sustained by the Church which cares for him to the very end. This care, too, is an inheritance from the Lord; so the Church represents the Lord to the individual and the individual is represented to the Lord. The Church represents both the Lord and the dying person to each other. The Church mediates, and in doing so uses what she possesses, her prayer here-and-now as well as her treasury of prayer, in order to prepare the dying man for the Lord's coming and to prepare his reception in the Lord's presence.

The Church is present in this twofold form because the Lord, in dying for all, has given his Bride a share in his death and his being reunited with the Father. Through the Church, his prayer and his words on the cross acquire a form which makes them accessible to all and valid for all; this is how the Church receives everything from the Lord in order to preserve and hand it on. She must know the hour of death's approach so that she can exercise her responsibility to God and the dying person, not only as an institution but as the living communion of saints. She administers the sacraments: the sacrament of the dying, in which, as it were, she gathers up the life of the dying person and renders it ecclesial, preparing it to meet the Father.

But in doing so she is also concerned with life's individual deeds: the dying man's confession is heard. In this final confession the Church tries to bring order into all that is as yet disordered. Indeed, the deathbed can even be the scene of a baptism, a confirmation or a marriage, in which the Church may have little to go on but the dying person's general consent and agreement. The Church acts so much on man's behalf that she even hears the Yes that was never expressly uttered, eliciting a fullness from it that she, the Church, brought to it. Thus, retroactively, she refashions a life, making it worthy of the Church, worthy of God. However much the Church disapproves of the Christian's neglect in postponing his decisions until the hour of death, she will not refuse him when that hour comes. This is because of the overflowing treasure of love that comes from the Lord on the cross, who wishes to die for every last human being and will not refuse the grace of his death to anyone.

The Church simply goes wherever the Lord is. She draws one final thing from his death in order to fashion eternal life out of it (together with him

who died in utter forsakenness, fulfilling the
Father's will, so that those who are his should not
be forsaken). From the very outset the Son had
promised the Father this one final thing; it was the
sign of his mission. In taking it over, the Church
assures the Son that she has laid hold of his mission. Furthermore, the Church must ratify it by becoming so alive and effective that she brings forth
fruit through and beyond the death of the individual, in a fruitfulness that comes from the
Father. On this basis the Church must give the
Father's creature back to him visibly marked by
the graces that flow from the Son's cross. The
Church does this, not only by calling on the Holy
Spirit, but by allowing the Spirit to dwell in her in
such a way that he looks after her fruitfulness.

Like all the other sacraments, the sacrament of
the dying has its effect when it is administered by
the Church. The Lord's power operates in the
administration of the sacrament, and it shows its
fullness by working not at a private level but at the
level of the Church, embracing both recipient and
minister, uniting the priest and the believer each
time in a new obligation. From the vast sum of
these obligations, everyone who participates in the
Church's treasury of prayer receives something.
Whenever a sacrament is administered there is a
direct effect that is communicated to the individual
recipient. But the indirect effect is no less at work;
it flows from the nature of the sacrament and also

from the nature of the communion of saints, that is, that influence of all the saints and martyrs who have lived and died for the Church, whose love was so bound to the Lord that they all died in that love. This love belonged to the triune God. He communicated it to the saints and martyrs in such a way that they were able to return it to him whole and entire, to be used by the Church in any way required, but chiefly for the production of saints who become such through their deaths. These are believers who attain to a perfect faith at the moment of death because this faith is no longer tested by their limitations and weaknesses of character, but has become of the Church, ecclesial; not in the sense of the mere institution but in the living sense in which the Spirit blows in the communion of saints. In all the sacraments, those who receive them are sent out by the Church: they are sent forth into the world, into life, into Church office or the religious state of life, into the vicissitudes of Christian existence. And in the sacraments of the dying, she sends them to God. They are enfolded in the Church's bosom, which anticipates the bosom of God.

When someone has died or is dying and the Church steps in with the consolation of word and sacrament, it is not only the dying person who feels a new indebtedness to the Church: the whole family, for the most part, shares in this sense of gratitude.

In the Church's purposeful intervention, the family sees a meaning it had not adequately grasped before. Not only the loneliness of the dying man, but also the isolation of those around him is breached by a higher instance that creates a new link with God. As the Lord was dying on the cross, a link was created between his Mother and John, but then the dying Lord's loneliness intensified: he experienced utter forsakenness. *Prior* to his death, the Church had to give way to a direct relationship between the Son and his Father. It may be that, in death, certain people have a complementary experience; having received the sacraments they become free and open to God in a new way. They draw near to him to the same degree that the Son experienced loneliness and abandonment, that is, in inverse proportions.

This opposition between the Son's intensifying loneliness and man's heightened fellowship with God shows how immense a burden the Father laid on his dying Son. The Father wanted the Son's mission to contain utter bitterness, total powerlessness, he wanted to stretch him beyond the limit, in order to be certain, as it were, that the immeasurability of human sin should find its place in the greater immeasurability of the passion. It was as if he wanted to show man that the Son is ever greater by unveiling the ever-greater dimensions of his suffering for sin. It is on the basis of this extreme grace that God permits many in the

Church to die peacefully, in a gentle return to God, in a feeling of security, of no longer wrangling with the inevitable.

So we come to see that the dying man, even if nothing extraordinary is required of him, is guaranteed a place in the Lord's dying; indeed, the Church can allot this place to him because of that freedom which permits the Bride to dispose of things that belong to the Bridegroom. This last place is always available for the person who is dying at any one moment; and only the Bride can take the liberty of so arranging things that everyone, in his turn, gets there. In a way, the Bride disregards the Lord's powerlessness in order to guarantee the believer the right that is his because of the Son's mission. Thus we see, therefore, that it is precisely when a man comes to die that the Church shows herself to be a prolongation of the Son's mission. The Son has given his completed mission back to the Father, but the Church continues to draw from it whatever she needs here and now.

Hence, in the Bride-Bridegroom relationship, a time has been created that is to the Church's advantage. There is a disproportion in the relationship that goes beyond all limits, and in transgressing all bounds of human propriety it gives us a glimpse of the triune relationships within God. In requiring something of the Son, the Father is absolutely inflexible. When God the Son desires the Spirit to come down upon the earth, he sets no humanly reasonable bounds to this desire. This is because the demands the sinner makes of God (even if the sinner is unaware of it) are always so great that they exceed all earthly measuring. The sinner's distance from God is so vast that reasonability is of no avail. Unless God's demands were divine in character, unless God's acts were insurpassable, each one surpassing the other, the work of redemption on the cross could be surpassed by man's negation. But when God makes demands of God he makes sure that God always overtakes man, that grace has more weight than sin, that the redemption is complete. The Church has no way of measuring what happens at any one time; all she knows, on the basis of her spousal relationship, is that the Bridegroom always does more, that his achievement has no end and that every believer, through the Church, may lay claim to it. In the Lord's dying there is a twofold boundlessness: what the Father asked of the Son, and what the Son has given to the Church.

Death is the entrance to eternal life. And in God's eternal life, all has been reconciled. All our measurements, our days and nights, our time and space, our abilities and assessments, have found their limitation in death. Now they may grow into the gift that God gives to those who are his, now they may open themselves anew to an eternal grace and become ready for life without end. As for the judgment and what comes between the moment of death and the opening of heaven, that too is contained in the relationship between Bride and Bridegroom, in what the Lord and the Church do together within the mystery of the Father, which results in the collapse of those barriers that each human being erects against infinite grace. The Church not only accompanies man to his death; she not only receives him, on the other side of judgment, at heaven's gate; she accompanies him from earth to heaven, and even the judgment introduces no interruption.

IX

DEATH AND THE SAINTS

When the Son says to someone, "Come, follow me", it is a summons to personal discipleship of him who comes from the Father and is on his way back to the Father. The one who receives this summons is given a mission, but it does not mean that he can know in advance to what he has bound himself, in terms of what it involves, its times and seasons. These take place in a sequence appointed by the Lord alone. Thus in giving his consent, he is vowing faithfulness; he expects his faith and the Lord to help him keep his vow. However, what he has vowed refers both to the Lord's earthly life and to his return to heaven. In other words, the substance from which he is to live his life is the substance of the Lord's own life, which is given to him at all times as the Lord sees best.

Now the one who has been sent, who has accepted his mission, must take his bearings completely from the Lord, aware that he will be living with demands that are too much for him, but that the Lord is keeping watch over him and his mission. It will involve everyday things, the absolving of certain duties common to all believers, but it will also involve (the unpredictable, things that may remain unintelligible right up to the end), or at best reveal their meaning only after years have gone by. He will have to do things which the Lord alone can assess, things designed to further his Church; he will have to be an instrument. Being an instrument applies not merely to things concerning the Church in this world, however: it applies to much that belongs to the mystery of heaven and is only brought to fulfillment there, things that can only be known and guided by the triune God.

So discipleship is a risk. But it is not like the risk a man takes when submitting to a high achievement test, for there is no way of seeing into God's level from the level of the world in which the Christian risk takes place, so there can be no evaluating of success. Thus a human being, constantly aware of his limitations, is expected to live a life that has none. As for marking stages and levels attained, reaching resting places from which to survey the distance traveled—all this is withdrawn from him. In any case, considering what the Lord is, he would not even want to evaluate his own achievements, for the relationship between merit and grace can never be reduced to a formula. No more can he calculate (what it means for the Son to be God and yet live as man. This relationship is the unattainable model held up to the disciple of Christ.) Without surrendering his reason, he is to confess a faith and live in a faith which is constantly going beyond it. This is a tension of grace, for the Lord, having lived out this tension in his divine–human way, imparts it to those who are his.

The world that exceeds our understanding and in which decisions are taken affecting practicing and praying Christians is the eternal world. Living on this earth, the man endowed with a mission determines to draw his nourishment from eternal life; he determines to take this infinity of God, this life (which, for him, signifies a life after death), as the decisive reality of his existence. He dies to this world in order to live, even now, on the basis of the other world, from which his bodily death as yet separates him. This death acquires an entirely new meaning for him. It will be the handing back of his mission, not the end of his life; for what is humanly speaking the end of his earthly life coincides with the moment when he vowed himself to the Lord. If man's life is characterized by his personal plans and their execution, by deeds and successes, the commissioned man has renounced this life. He allows others to plan for him; he turns his back on success; he ceases to be the person he was. This renunciation signifies a death that has occurred prematurely, and this death, in turn, signals advance permission to live according to the laws of eternal life.

However, these laws of eternity are given by

God; they cannot be grasped in the form of a table of laws but only by love. They are fashioned by love, and the human being to whom they are addressed should live constantly in love in such a way that he experiences them as such. In fact, he should love as the Son loved mankind and, loving, experienced love's laws. Love alone enabled the Son to live as a man among men; love alone enabled him, as man, to find words to speak to men's hearts, to express Christian teaching, to show men something of eternal life and to give them a share in the triune love. And just as love brought the Son to the world without his forfeiting the vision of the Father, so now it is love, in faith, that must enable the Lord's disciple to grasp the love of heaven without forfeiting his own human nature, without condemning the world, without separating himself from his fellow men and excluding them.

So this love must be in a position to sow new life on the earth; the sower must take what he has experienced of the divine and communicate it to his fellow men in a way they can understand, in a compelling way. He can do this only if he himself is completely transparent so that the word of God is not split as it passes through him, if he passes on the substance of this word—love—intact, whether by living in love among men or by dwelling in love in a house of pure prayer, dedicating to the world his prayer of love and his fruitfulness.

Through his Yes he has taken up a position of mediation between heaven and earth. And his Yes comes from the Son's mission, for the Son not only lived out his mediatorship in its divine-human uniqueness: he also offered it in sacrifice and communicated it to others.

From now on, everything that happens in the life of the commissioned person will be marked by the sign of God's love, even the things he cannot grasp, even the things that necessarily underline his loneliness and forsakenness, with the result that he may no longer interpret his fellowship with human beings in any other way but as fellowship with God. In his neighbor, therefore, he sees the Lord; he seeks the Lord in him. He sees the Lord's brother in him rather than the sinner (perhaps the sinner who is persecuting him), rather than a fellow man encumbered with a thousand impediments. In this way God can use him as appropriate; he can adopt not only his human life but each of his sufferings, and his death, into the transformation and fruitfulness of eternal life.

Bodily death is not an isolated phenomenon. By making inroads into man, death prepares him to leave this world for the world of eternity. The death of a religious, of a saint, willed, affirmed and consented to by him, is a free act that allows us to hear God's answer. If he goes on living in the world to which he no longer belongs, perhaps accustoming himself to a life of renunciation in a monastery, earthly goods of all kinds will once again be heaped up around him: new habits, new manners and new graces. If his original renunciation was not entirely in earnest, he will be in danger, all too soon, of making his cell into a world of its own and his renunciation into a new greed. Perhaps only the saint can renounce everything without always being on the lookout for a return and settling down again in a new environment. At any rate, there remains a difference between the death of the ordinary Christian and that of the vowed person and the saint. The saint renounces in order to insert himself into the will of God, so that it may always be his highest aim. For him, death according to God's Will is the highest gift God has prepared for him, for he has no doubt about this Will. He does not doubt that the Father has prepared his heaven, through the Son's sacrifice, for those who are his.

Within this absolute consent there can be the most varied decisions and developments. Precisely because God can (and does) make his saints into instruments of his Will, he challenges them, in all personal areas, with things that can only be borne in faith and in the context of God's being ever greater. For instance, the death of Thérèse of Lisieux is a difficult one; she feels it approaching and wants to correspond completely with the Father's Will, but she cannot muster up the strength to utter a joyful Yes. It is as if, at the very crowning of her mission, the Father permits her this gentle uncertainty as a foil to the perfect certainty of other saints who unhesitatingly embrace death (of whatever kind) as coming from God. And when Joan of Arc recants in the attempt to save her life, we see God allowing much in her life to remain human, bound to the environment she loved, her native soil; we see him allowing the flesh to know a weakness that will cause the spirit a moment's vacillation. And while Ignatius clearly sees his end before him, he does not succeed in convincing his friends of it. He cannot find the words to move them to send in time for the papal blessing for which he longs. He alone has said his full Yes, while his companions are still hesitating.

Whatever the death of the individual saint may look like, it must serve to interpret the Lord's death. The mystery of loneliness, forsakenness and rejection in the Lord's death is so fruitful that God cannot do otherwise than allow his saints to taste something of it. Somewhere there must be an evident hiatus between the whole line of the saint's life and dedication and the moment of his death, so that the Christian doctrine may be better understood and so that, on all sides, the event that took place in the heart of the dying Son may be re-activated in the Father's presence. In this way, what took place at the center, in the Son, can manifest itself at the periphery, through the death of the saints who followed him, proving fruitful for believers and those who are seeking faith.

If we could find out what is going on in the heart of the triune God at the moment when the Son dies on the cross, we would encounter a love that is of infinite significance for mankind, that finally brings man home; for here God loved the world so much that he gave up his only Son. He seems to have preferred man to God himself; he seems to have felt such love for his creature that there is no room left for the divine love. There is no room left: after his death the Son of Man will first descend to the underworld. This descent, which in the Son's case follows his death, takes place prior to death in the case of the saint, at whatever time God decrees, but at all events it must end no later than the moment of death itself. By the time he meets the Father, every covering must have fallen away; by this time also, however, his earthly mission should have reached its greatest fruitfulness. The saint's heavenly mission is to be fashioned out of his earthly fruitfulness; when we in the world call upon the saint, when he works miracles and hears prayers, (these powers he uses—which are ultimately divine powers—were gathered on earth.) On earth they were so woven into the saint's divinely willed holiness that now, in heaven, he can wield them. Here, for the saint, death signifies a caesura, putting an end to any suffering,

whereas in the Son's case—and in his case alone—
it leaves room for his journey to the underworld.

The Son's coming to earth fulfills every one of the
Old Covenant promises. In a divine way he lives
out every fulfillment. Every step he takes fulfills
something. We, as believers, are invited to see and
ponder this fulfillment in everything, to participate,
in faith, in all that he does. We are not merely to
make some general act of belief within the Church
as instituted by him: we are meant to share the
experience of fulfillment together with the Son.
Every word he speaks brings some fulfillment; it
vitally affects our Christian life by necessarily
presupposing and linking up with other events.
Thus every word shares in the entirety of doctrine.
Conversely, however, the entirety of doctrine is
found in each word.

The believer who lives as a mediocre Christian
develops the habit of preferring some aspects of
his life of faith and obscuring others. He does this
lest he should suddenly be obliged to face realities
that are beyond his grasp, that would stretch him
beyond his limits and overwhelm him; his whole
existence might be called into question by the
transformation of values they would imply. In the
case of the saint, things are different. He, by
contrast, embraces in his realities particularly those
things he finds most shattering, which rob him of
his security, which keep him in suspense; in fact he

prefers those things which seem incredible, those things which, even to faith, surpass faith. For him the fulfillment of promises is not restricted to the Lord's historical life and his relationship to the Old Covenant; it does not merely give earthly confirmation of the old prophecies by showing them to have come true. For him it is something here and now, something beyond inspection and verification. It includes the promises referring to heavenly life, and above all, the Lord's promises regarding what he has in store for us in heaven.

For the saint, this heaven is not a future event (as the New Covenant was for the Jews). For he himself takes part in its fulfillment. He lives in the certainty of eternity. This does not mean that he cannot feel a certain anxiety—his weaknesses may appear as big as sins to him; he can feel not only reverence but also proper fear of God and his judgment. But he is so aware of eternity's triumph over transience that his truth really lives in heaven; not only does he continually have recourse to it, he is privileged to regard it as his daily bread. To him, truth resides in the triune God, and this is so real to him that the everyday, visible experience of the senses acquires an almost vague outline. At any rate, it loses some of its importance and remains meaningful only where there is a discernible connection with the Lord's commandment of love and the life of heaven.

The saint sets aside none of the commandments

the Lord has given him (and every believer) for this life, but he regards everything as provisional: it sets the direction, but has already been surpassed by the Lord, and only in heaven will it achieve completeness. Heaven's truth is continually intervening to transform the truth of his everyday life. The risk which the saint takes lies far less in his renunciation of the things of this world than in the fact that he puts himself perfectly at heaven's disposal and endeavors to see traces of the Eternal One in everything that happens to him here below. These traces demonstrate to him—both objectively and subjectively—the ever-greater reality of heaven. So death, which he sees before him, is the open door leading from the earthly risk into the heavenly. He has no fear that there may be nothing behind the door or only disappointment. He knows with certainty that he will find infinitely more than he could ever have expected, since the relation of heaven's fulfillment to the earth is far greater than that of the New Covenant to the Old. God is ever greater; this is a reality that will not cease being fulfilled for all eternity.

In the mystery of the relation between nature and supernature, the saint knows the power of supernature, measured against the power of nature. It is not merely superordinate, it is a divine mystery that God has always bestowed upon those who are his. Nature could be compared to a human conversation which, through the sudden intervention of a divine voice, is not merely interrupted, not merely supplemented, but elevated to an entirely different and unimaginable level: it becomes a participation in the conversation of the Trinity in heaven.

And now the saint is about to die as a man. His nature has received such injuries that he dies. In the process of dying, he may experience fear and pain to such an extent that the Yes of his consent may be inaudible, and he may cease to understand. But that is not essential, for supernature has so enveloped his nature that God does not cease to hear the response of his Yes to his mission (which is equivalent to his holiness). He is completely taken up to God's plane, even in cases where a human observer, and perhaps the saint himself, can no longer discern anything of the divine.

We are again offered a comparison with the life of the Church, which is full of human inadequacy and can give rise to scandal at every turn because of the weakness of individuals (both laypeople and priests) and because of the ossification of a hierarchy that is no longer in any way like a ladder leading up to heaven. Yet the Church lives on the basis of the supernature imparted to her by the Son, a supernature that is above all nature and all time. The Church remains holy even where the individual fails, where faulty understandings and errors creep in, just as the saint remains holy even where the humanly observable signs of his holiness have been completely taken up into God, even where, in order to humble him even more, he seems to have lost the thread of dialogue with God. No one who had merely observed the last hours of Thérèse of Lisieux would have dreamed of calling her a saint on the basis of those hours. And yet these hours are entirely holy, for they reach back to her everyday life of holiness and are prolonged to the level of that only valid Yes that is unceasingly uttered by God.

When the Son dies on the cross, he dies the death of all sinners and all saints. For all the dead, the moment of his death signals a transference to the eternal plane, a transference that will be tangible to all since the Lord has redeemed everyone by his death. Thus his death has acquired a particular meaning for each person. No one can turn away from it as if it were unimportant, or as if it were something he had long ago seen through, that no longer holds any secrets for him. It is the Lord's death, of vital relevance at every moment. It so refashions and transforms every other death, assuming it into itself, that as far as the individual is concerned it is no longer his own death that is important but the Lord's, surrounded as it is by the whole mystery of the triune God, by the Father's will which allowed the Son to die in this way. Henceforth every man knows that his death is not merely contained in the Lord's death, but has a direct relation to the Father. This is not the Old Testament relationship, where the Father appointed death as a punishment, and everything that was to take place after death was removed from sight. Now the Father of the New Covenant is manifest through the Son's death. Becoming man, the Son proclaims the Father's will to create a new way of access to heaven. And apparently this will refers entirely to the earth, to man's earthly conversion.

On the cross, however, the Son's earthly life comes to an end; but the Eternal Father who permitted the redemption stands behind it, so that, for believers, even what comes after death is kept safe in God. In fact, the Father's grace in the New Covenant begins to unveil itself fully at the moment when the crucified Son can no longer find him. Not only because the Father is now withdrawing from him, but—as the Son's resurrection will show—because the Father is so much involved with human beings that he even causes his own Son to rise from the dead as a man. He receives back the Son's mission, which goes far beyond earthly life, in such a way that it contains all the human beings of his creation. At the point where the Son gives back his mission and the Spirit, Father and Son take up responsibility for what is to come. No longer is it only the Son who effects the transformation of death, but the Son in the will of the Father and the love of the Spirit.

This refashioning of death, which casts its shadow in advance in the Son's renunciation of power over his own life—a renunciation taken up by those under vows, the disciples of Jesus—signifies a revaluation of the whole of existence. From now on eternity's goals can be pursued on earth; death can begin at the same place as spiritual renunciation. Now bodily dying is only something that man has to undergo as a physical being. However, the Son suffers for our sins, and at the same time he suffers for the sake of the missions of saints yet to come. He does this by imparting an actuality to his suffering that can take effect in the life of every believer, not only as a symbol but as the power which makes discipleship possible. And as for the saint who loves the Lord enough to give his life for him, who is ready to renounce everything for the sake of his grace, who, out of reverence for the triune God, wants nothing more of God than to be put wherever he can be of service, he is privileged to be allowed to assist at the Lord's death in a way the Lord himself determines. He is allowed to help the Lord carry the sins of mankind and complete his work in the midst of being forsaken by the Father.

The Church celebrates the feasts of the Lord in a regular sequence; with her characteristic institutional objectivity, she gives each one its particular stamp, taking what is the Lord's and handing it on according to his wishes. But the vitality of what happens in the Church is guaranteed, not by the fact that the Lord is always present in the Church and her celebrations, but by his saints constantly suffering anew with him, at a time appointed by God independently of the calendar (or maybe related to it). The regularity of Church life is continually being interrupted by the actuality of the life of her saints, albeit this life of theirs mostly remains hidden until they die. Sanctity takes its ultimate secret with it to the grave, just as the Lord took the ultimate mystery of his Sonship with him to his death so that the Father should cause him to rise again. The saints are almost always recognized after they have died, when the Church is able to take their being into her own system, when she is able to master their qualities, their teachings, their mysteries in such a way as to render them profitable to others. It is by being used by the Church for her purposes (and mostly long after he has died) that the saint acquires a visible significance in the Church; whereas, while he dwelt on the earth, this meaning remained a secret between him and God. This reveals a new aspect in the Lord's words about not knowing the hour of his own death: it refers to the saints' vital influence in the Church and to the fact that their secret remains veiled and is kept safe in God and must become fruitful in God so that the Church can recognize it. Unless a grain of wheat falls into the earth and dies. . .

X

ANOINTING FOR DEATH

The sacraments are arranged around the cross. They are closely related to the Lord's death and hence, since he dies our death, to our deaths also. And since the Lord creates the Church to assist in the salvation of the world, and makes her into his Bride, we must see the Church in the closest connection with his death. He dies so that we may live, and since he gives us his entire life, our death is fundamentally transformed: we die so that we may live through him. We sinners die in order to become saints; we earthly people die in order to become heavenly. The Church is no mere institution, however; she is the Lord's living Bride, receiving her life from him, a life that is not only given away but is also *experienced* as life. All that the Lord has undergone, all he has gathered together so that it may not be lost, so that every trace of his life shall have its own significance, a life-transforming significance: this is what the Church administers. In administering sacraments, she is passing on the Lord's life experiences of the most diverse kinds. Even his experience of death is ultimately a life experience of this kind: the experience of surrendering his earthly life to heaven, of breaking off his existence among us in order to live an eternal resurrection life in heaven.

If, marked with the sign of death, sick and dying as we are, we look upon the Lord's cross, we can draw from it not only an insight into his entire life but also a conclusive understanding of our own Christian life, a life which the Church continually gives us afresh, during our transitory life, in the form of sacraments. It may be that we have paid it scant attention, that we have rarely become aware of the whole breadth and depth of experience it contains. Now, in death, we realize that we have been equipped for life; in the Church's sacrament—in the sacrament of the dying as in all the sacraments—we have been given what is most essential for our heavenly life in a form instituted and hallowed by the Lord. By this form he will recognize us as his own. And as for the judgment and the purification we have to go through, we see them not only as things promised us by the Lord, but also as prolongations, extensions of the Church's sacraments, not to cause us to perish but, on the contrary, to prepare us, brought and kept alive by the Church's sacraments, for the life of eternity.

The recipient of the anointing of the sick is signed with the sign of death, a death that is both given to him and taken away from him. It is *given* by the Lord since the Lord dies the sinner's death; it is *taken away* from him since the sinner should have died a death quite different from the one he actually died. This giving and taking away, which is designed to empower the believer no longer to live his natural life but that of a believer whom the Lord will redeem and has already redeemed, is the grace of the Lord's earthly life, which he is constantly bestowing on those who are his. From before all time he, the Son, is the Anointed One, for even when, in eternity, he decides upon his incarnation, he makes the acquaintance of his death. This death accompanied him during the Old Covenant until he became truth on the cross. The Son appears as the Father's Anointed, the One who comes into the world to die, with the Father's agreement. His death is so full of significance that even the promises of the prophets refer to him as the Anointed One. He will live and he will die, and in both he will offer his existence in sacrifice to the Father. In birth and life he will fulfill the meaning of the Father's creation, in suffering and dying he will carry out the meaning of his Father's punishment. For the Son does not come as a second Adam to fulfill creation only as far as the Fall; rather he comes in order to lift it up again at the point where the creature failed.

Thus the Father recognizes the Godhead in this Redeemer, but also the manhood, for the Redeemer bears the sins as if they were his own. He follows the path of mankind right up to the point where man let go of the Father's hand, right up to the imposition of punishment. He makes no exception, he will take the whole destiny upon himself. In this, from the very outset, he is the Anointed One, the One ordained to be a perfect sacrifice. The anointing includes his essential relationship both to the Father and to man: as the Father's Son he wants to lay his whole existence on the line in order to bear the guilt of all men. His will is in accordance with the Father's will: he does what the Father expects. He also does what men expect, what complete fulfillment of the promise implies. For through him they will be converted, they will receive the full Christian faith and will have to be ready, out of obedience to the Father, to do for the Son whatever is expected of them. When Mary of Bethany anoints him, she fulfills his expectation, but she also manifests the obedience which believers are to offer him. In a manner of speaking, she manifests this obedience over the Son's head and to the Father, who, through her act of anointing, can recognize his Son as the genuine man, the One anointed for his task.

Thus a whole circle is drawn around the anointed Son, the circle of mankind that shares in his work; and not only sinful mankind either, turned away from him and crucifying him, but also dedicated mankind, which performs on the Son, in faith, that sign which the Father expects. So when we die the Father will not only see us as those whom the Son has signed: he will see the Son as the One we have signed. It is on the basis of his having been signed by us that the Son goes on to sign those who are his own, for the Son accepts the anointing performed on him as a sacramental anointing, carried out by Mary as representing the Church. He appears here in the role of beneficiary in his relation to the Church. He becomes so completely man with a view to the cross that he allows himself to be anointed by the Church at the very moment when he gives anointing to the Church and empowers her to anoint us with the sign of the Son—so that the Father shall recognize us. The Son gives us everything, but in being anointed he also takes something from us, fashioning a point of connection, welding himself forever to the Church. It is like the ring which the bridegroom receives from the bride. Just as she desires to bear his imprint in everything, he too, mortal, dying for her, wishes to carry her memento.

The best image of death found in the New Covenant is that of the Lord's birth. It signifies the end of the Old Covenant and yet gathers up its inner life, everything that God regarded as important, and brings it over into the New, creating a New Covenant out of the new life. Under the Old Covenant, the Jews lived under the gaze of a Father who continually promised the Son's coming. This promise was more or less clearly visible down through the ages. It was never so entirely absent that, as

Christian observers, we can look back and say that at this or that point the Jews were abandoned, or were shown only the Father's severity, not his mercy. There was hope in the reception of the Law, in the keeping of the commandments; everywhere there were signs of promise, but they never became concrete reality for believers. For *promise* means that the fulfillment will only be granted to later generations.

So the Jews are obliged to live under a concrete covenant with the Father, while clinging to the promise of a fulfillment they cannot envisage. Their existence is referred to a truth which is so hidden in God's counsel that they can do nothing to substantiate it. They cannot even live in it: in order to go on living, they must hold primarily to what has taken place, what has, after all, become clear. Once the Son appears, the promise breaks off, for the fulfillment has come. But the promise contained so much that the Christian who lives in the fulfillment can and must continually return to the promise. By doing so he will be able to live the present better, grasp the various aspects of Christian teaching more profoundly and be continually and freshly overwhelmed by the triune God's infinite possibilities of acting on earth.

Thus the Christian lives on earth in the fulfillment of a promise, in a reality that *is* his world, in the Church and in the Christian teaching. But all this too is a promise looking toward eternity.

Therefore while he is on the hither side he has to live with a view to what is yonder; in the transitory world he has to look for traces of the eternal world. In this way he will give his life the substance which the triune God would like to find realized there. Like his brother under the Old Covenant, he lives only partly in the concrete world; he lives predominantly in the life of the coming eternity, which exceeds his grasp. The ultimate reality of this life lies in God's infinity. As far as the individual aspects of eternal life are concerned, he can plumb them as little as the Jew could grasp the concrete realization of prophecy.

The Son comes from eternity and returns there after his temporal existence. His human existence is embedded in his eternal being. He endures it not only because he enjoys the vision of the eternal Father, but primarily out of love: love for the Father and for us. In him, this love which faces in two directions is always in perfect unity. So we can regard the Son's eternity as a truth that situates our life together with his in a time span between the eternity that is past and the eternity which is to come. It follows from this that every truth concerning eternity is important for our present existence even if we cannot fully grasp it. Each of these truths enables us to focus so on the actuality of eternal truth, to sharpen its presence in us, that we can already live our lives on the basis of its eternal meaning. Moreover, we must so cling to it that we also die in it.

The person who wishes to give his life totally to the Lord has to die to this world, it is true; but ultimately he cannot act as if it did not exist. It contains realities—even were they only things concerning the redemption—which have to acquire crucial significance for his life. So he must bear and endure the real world within his renunciation and sacrifice, he must bring it with him as a living reality so that God may refashion it. He dies to the world, but the world has not died to him. If he wanted to shut himself up in a contemplative life known only to God, turned away from the world's needs, suffering and distress, he could not be considered a Christian, for his love would not be an image of the Son's two-directional love. His so-called love of God would be much more like an infringement of the commandment of neighborly love. But even in pure contemplation he has the opportunity, through the sufferings he frequently has to bear and through his life of penance, to draw the world into his self-offering to God. He is called to imitate the Son's sacrifice; he must perform his dying to the world (and to everything in it of which he was fond) in and together with the Lord's death, in order to attain that power of coredemption that can present the world afresh to the Father.

Thus the Old Covenant must die because it was a promise; it must end where the fulfillment begins. Similarly, the human being who is already living here below in virtue of eternal life must have died to this earth. However, just as the New Covenant is built upon the foundations of the Old, the Christian's eternal life is built on the foundations of his earthly life (even in the case of the strictest contemplative life); that is precisely how it becomes a sharing of the Lord's life.

Yet the Son brings death with him in a further way. By entering into time he becomes nothing, he renounces his heavenly life (without losing his vision of the Father): this is a death. Even his birth contains a premonition of the cross. And it is clear that those who wish to follow him must include in their self-dedication that renunciation which the Son performs at his birth. He undergoes a twofold death to redeem the world: he bids farewell to the Father and to his beloved heaven in order to address himself to the world's need, in order to cultivate his vision of the Father in a way which includes the perspectives of earth, and in order, finally, to die on the cross totally forsaken by the Father, presenting the perfect sacrifice of his life for sinners. He dies in alienation and rejection, but he dies for love's sake, for a love which he bequeaths to men in the form of a commandment, a love he continually squanders on them, to such an extent that it produces their faith, their whole Christian life.

Everything he does shows them what they have to do. From contemplating his life among them and in the Father's presence, they can draw the entire substance of Christian teaching. For not for a moment is this teaching abstract: it is teaching for life through and through, and the experience of death is an essential part of it.

At one time death was a punishment taking place between the sinner and God the Father. Death's severity was all the more acute because what followed it was veiled from sight. In taking away the veil the Son renders death less terrible. This gain applies not only to eternal life; it takes effect, partially, in everyday life on earth in terms of discipleship, that is, the life of prayer, the search for the triune God and love in imitation of the Son's love. It is a love that is lifted up by the triune God, right from the start, to the heights of heaven; it is not isolated and lonely, but privileged to share in the triune life of love. It is a love that God receives because he gave it in the first place and recognizes it, and because he sees that it bears the sign of the Anointed Son, just as he recognizes the Son's anointing in every anointing carried out in his name.

In the Church the one who anoints is himself anointed; at priestly ordination his hands were anointed, recalling and strengthening the baptismal anointing in which the Christian, stepping into life, was initiated into Christ's death. (Thus baptismal anointing points ahead to the anointing of the sacrament of the dying.) However, the priestly anointing is not to make him an anointed one like the Lord, but to make him a minister of anointing. He himself bears the sign of death, but he imparts ultimate meaning to the death of those entrusted to him. He anoints them for life, a life that is and remains the Lord's life because it is eternal life; dying, the Christian is privileged to enter it. The priest who anoints the dying man is standing where Christ stood when he brought men, through his death, into eternal life. He too, together with Christ, has been anointed for death by the Church.

When God divided night from day he gave men the power of number. And when he banished mortal men from paradise, numbers acquired a relation to men's transience. They had to live in a time that was running out, and this signified both a punishment and a blessing. A punishment, because everything they did was doomed to perish. And while they hoped to achieve something lasting, something that would survive, even something eternal, they had to recognize that eternity was reserved to God and that their works shared their transitory nature to an extent that was beyond their power of finding out. Not only had they to leave unfinished some work they had begun, they had to consign this inchoate project to uncertainty;

it would be affected by transience in some form or
other.

When the Son came into the world he brought
things with him that were eternal, not only eternal
divine truth, which rendered men's span of time in
this world bearable once more since they could
turn to the eternal God in a new way, but also
divine life, which he gave them in order to open
them up for eternal things and prepare them for a
life in eternity. And in making the Church into a
Bride who would go on living after his earthly life,
he gave those who would live in her a new time
span, superior to the transitory time of creation
and sin. Living in this new time span, they could
receive goods that come from eternity and promises
referring to an eternity that is future. The very fact
that a Christian dies in the Church means that his
death does not merely bear the stigma of transitoriness: it is the Christian's entry into an eternity in
which, through the Church, he already has a share.

Now the anointing enables the dying man to
accompany the Lord to the Father, to share in the
mystery of his resurrection and ascension. Through
the Church, earthly existence acquires a quality
that orientates it to participation in God's eternity
and infinity. Man's work too, justified by God, is
enabled to enter into eternity. And if the Christian
labors and endeavors to act in an apostolic way, he
knows that transience cannot affect his work, no

more than the passing nature of the Son's earthly
days can affect his work on earth, together with
what they have achieved, they both return to
God's eternity. If man succeeded in thinking only
of eternity, he would see nothing in death but the
transition to it. He would consent in advance to
everything God had in store for him because it
would signify his purification and preparation for
eternity. The more he is entangled in transitory
things, however, the harder death is for him. He is
reluctant to leave those who are close to him,
although he knows that they will die after him. He
is loath to leave his work, although he knows that
it will perish. He feels that he is indispensable on
earth. Once he has received the sacraments of the
dying, however, the bright colors of this world
finally fade. He may have made little room for
faith during his life, but now he knows that he has
received something that has nothing to do with his
transitory nature, something that empowers him
to undergo death as a transition to eternity.

In her treasury of prayer, the Church has a wealth
of answered prayer which will support the dying
man, a wealth of revealed truths full of a wisdom
that comes to her directly from the Son's eternal life
and is available to all the Church's members. The
Church, as Bride, can bring forth things from her
bridal mystery and give them to the dying man so
that, thus appareled, he will be seen in the light of
eternity as a genuine child of the Church not only

by the Bridegroom, but also by the Father and the Spirit.

In creation, the Father creates out of what is most his own in order to fashion his world. Consequently there is a direct encounter between the creature and God, not only at the general end of the world but also at the death of every believer. All that preceded it in terms of personal destiny, but also everything the world was, everything providence had planned for the world, all that had been carried out or had remained inchoate, all that was sin—all this has come to its end in death. Nor is it a terrible end in the face of a wrathful Creator, for the world's Redeemer holds the judgment in his hand, he who has suffered so much for every individual that there is room for everyone in his redemption. The Son is that creature who, at his death, put himself and his whole being into the hands of the Creator, and through him these same hands are open, once for all, in a gesture of welcome. At the point where, for every creature, the world comes to an end, it falls, not into the void, but into God. God gave it, now he takes it back to himself. But in everyone who thus returns to him, God recognizes the marks of his Son's earthly life. He recognizes his sacrifice, his sufferings and (inseparable from them) his love, that love that made his earthly path possible and fashioned his resurrection into a feast of the triune, divine love, a feast of unity undivided and restored, to which man too can claim admittance through the Son's being. Now the commandment to love our neighbor that the Son left us shows itself to be a claim to eternal life: thus man became qualified to share in the life of eternity.

Paul says, "Now abide these three, but the greatest of these is love." By the grace of the Son, man possessed faith and the hope which fulfilled it. And if these two were not great enough to endure beyond time, there is still love, which is the love of Christ, growing in each person so much that it brings about the sinner's justification and accompanies him, through the judgment, into eternity; it is the unbroken, divine love that is given to man. I believe as best I can; I hope as best I can; I love, finally, as best I can. But the Son's love—and in it the love of the triune God—is infinite, accompanying the dying through death and leading them to their place in eternal life.

XI

MARY'S DEATH

The great mystery of the Lord's Mother is the mystery of surrender. It is a surrender that belongs totally to the triune God: to the Father, who gives her her Son; to the Spirit, who overshadows her; and to the Son, who allows himself to be carried by her. But since she is a human being, living completely in the triune mystery of the Son's incarnation, she belongs from the first to those who keep the commandment of neighborly love. She loves man and God with a love that is transmitted directly through the Son and that belongs to her along with the promise. Just as she fulfills the promise, so too she fulfills love. This mystery of hers is rooted in her preredemption. In so far as she is redeemed in advance, immaculately conceived, a human being kept free of original sin through the Son's grace, she has no part in death. If, in spite of this, she dies, it is by way of imitating what the Son does. She is not excluded from death since the Son himself has died. Her death can only be understood in connection with his. For her, death is not the implementing of a

necessary punishment for sin; hence it can only be
part of her perfect love's fulfillment.

The Son loved men to the extent of dying on the
cross for them. Through the Son, the Mother
loves them to such an extent that she too dies a
human death. But the Son has not only brought
men redemption, which makes his Mother a co-
redemptrix. He has also brought men eternal life,
life in the vision of the Father together with the
Son and Spirit in eternity. His Mother shares in
this gift of eternity right from the outset, with the
result that in her case there is no need for any
moment to interpose itself between death and
eternity. She is not brought to any judgment; the
moment of her death immediately passes over into
the moment of her assumption into heaven. She
needs no purification; she does not need to turn
away from her past life; there is no need of any
sentence, any separation of good from evil. She
can be assumed just as she is. Not merely because
she has been preredeemed and her destiny has
unrolled in isolation from that of other human
beings, but equally because she desired to com-
mune with them right to the end—and on the
other hand because the Father has given the Son
this gift, namely, that his Mother should be assumed into heaven just as he was at his ascension.

When the Son rose from the dead, the women
found the stone rolled away by angels. Evidently a
release had taken place between the sealed tomb

and the scene in the garden. This was a first school in the idea of resurrection for sinners who are hard of understanding. Later the Lord appears to the assembled disciples behind closed doors: now there is no need for external obstacles to be shifted away. In the forty days following Easter, he enjoys fellowship with the disciples in the mystery of a bodily presence that obeys different laws than before the cross. This was the second school. The disciples could accustom themselves to all these new things: they listened to his word, spoke with him, followed his instructions, until his ascension put an end to this mode of existence too. The Mother does not skip these forty days, nor the ascension (which she did not need), any more than the sign of the empty tomb. As soon as she dies she is assumed bodily into heaven. The body which bore the Son, the hands that cared for him, the Virgin's countenance he knew on earth, her whole appearance as he saw her in the house in Nazareth and as the apostles knew her, her whole being as God created it so that it should be worthy of the Son—all this is now seen to be worthy of eternal life.

Thus the Son's meeting with his Mother in heaven is a reunion with her whom he had always known, known not only as God, from before all time, but also humanly, as a man. Through the presence of his Mother, the mystery of his own incarnation acquires a new form of duration in the eternal realm. The Son was God from eternity and has returned to the Godhead, which is his by right. But his Mother brings a piece of earth and world and humanity with her, a prolongation of what the Son was on earth; so she continues the fulfillment of her own promise, exploding all temporal barriers in a movement that assumes the finite into the infinite. All the restrictions God imposed on man through the transitory nature of his body are lifted because the spotless Mother is not subject to the law of sin, and even more because the Son, who continues to live bodily in his earthly Church, also needs his Church to have a corporal existence in heaven.

The Son made his Mother into his Bride, and she was so immaculate that nothing could stop her from living together with him in heaven in the same life she possessed on earth, a life that has now become universal because it characterizes the life of the Church in heaven. She, the Virgin who became the Lord's Mother, the Bride who is the Church of the Bridegroom, enters heaven with that body which sufficed on earth to make her the mediatrix of graces. She retains the body which bore the Son and was the dwelling place of her soul and spirit, in an immediacy which all heaven experiences and which, precisely *as* immediacy, signifies and confirms the bodily resurrection for all other human beings and for the whole Church. The Son slowly prepared his disciples for faith in his resurrection, from the empty tomb, via the closed doors and up to his ascension; now, without any intermediate stages, he can suddenly propose faith in his Mother's assumption. She embodies the mystery of the Church which dwells bodily in heaven, just as the eucharistic and heavenly Lord dwells bodily on earth.

From the very start the Mother's body was wrapped in the promise, growing in it, and in it she carried the Son. But when she comes to die, she first of all dies a bodily death in fellowship with all who die, with all human beings who have incurred punishment. She herself has no guilt, no more than the Son endured death on the cross because of personal guilt. But she dies not merely in fellowship with the guilty but also in fellowship with her Son, bound to him, sharing in his mission. Under the Old Covenant, when a prophet was sent, he was identified with his mission body and soul, even though his body received no special distinction on that account. The body of the Lord and that of his Mother, however, bear the stigmata of their mission; the Son's body, by coming into the world from heaven, the Mother's by receiving this seed from the Holy Spirit through a spiritual consent. The Son causes the mission of his body to be continued through the Eucharist, and he gives his Mother a share in this continuing bodily mission by taking her bodily into heaven. This mysterious continuance of the body in the eternal realm is essential, to mould the Church as a bodily reality and also to impress on Christians the importance of their earthly existence.

Under the Old Covenant death was the end; what came after it was a closely guarded secret, jealously kept by God as his own. By the time of the Son and his Mother, this secret had been opened up to some extent in various ways, and if after their death it seems to have adopted a more implacable aspect once more, this is only because the faith of those who came after was not strong enough, because they did not have the courage to face the mystery of the Son's ascension and his Mother's bodily assumption and go on facing it. For the Christian life is not merely the implementation of teaching delivered by the Son, adapted and limited to the needs of time and space; it stretches out to the mystery of eternity. (The believer always has the right to see all his actions under the light of eternity and to expect it to be thus clarified.) He no longer needs to take his limitations and his transitory nature as immutably given; here and now he can live—in advance, so to speak—on the basis of eternal things. Nor is this "advance" granted to him sparingly. He need not be afraid: in stamping his transitory, temporal existence with the mark of eternal duration he will not be doing anything inappropriate or unlawful, for both Son and Mother have entrusted him with the mystery of their death and resurrection, which are so intertwined that the unity they manifest applies to him too.

The believer may not approach the tasks of his life here below solely with earthly considerations and perspectives; nor may he put earthly limits on his Christian hope and love—even in matters that seem to be purely human. For he is a citizen of heaven, and his citizenship is one of love. This love, lived out by the Son and his Mother, became so fruitful that the lives of all of us are marked by this mystery. Its fruitfulness was such that life and death must seem a gift of God; we must see them together, as a unity, so that we may experience something of what Mother and Son have experienced on earth and in heaven. We are not to be struck merely by isolated details of their lives; rather, we are to grasp their whole inseparably earthly-and-eternal being as the revelation of a single, triune mystery.

When Mary says to the angel, "Let it be to me according to your word", she allows herself to enter into and become one with the word. She wants the word to put forth its power. And the Word is the Son. She is aware of the greatness of the promise, but not for a moment is she disturbed by the fact that *she* is the chosen one. She does not try to be so conscious of the grace of her position as to attract merit; she simply lets the Word take place. She is only the being in whom it takes place, in whom the Word becomes human life in order to dwell among us.

Mary says Yes to a love, but she says Yes out of love. And at this moment she does not suspect that this love is the greatest thing she can do. She does not suspect that, for all ages, she will never stop loving; that her life, up to now kept safe in the love of the triune God and her neighbor, will from now on become a vessel pouring forth nothing but love, spreading out in all directions, constantly growing, constantly being taken up into the greatest reality of all. Suddenly she is no longer the young, almost unknown girl whose life still belonged to the Old Covenant; she has become the bearer, the cofounder of the New Covenant. Solely out of love. The Son redeemed her in advance, from all eternity; therein lay the sign of his love, but also its fruitfulness. And now, when she responds to his love, she does so with a fruitfulness which he has given her and which will suffice for all Christian generations. She will bear him, humanly, because he has resolved, divinely, to be humanly born. She will give birth to him because he chose her for that purpose. She does not draw any personal profit from her election; thus she can be free, free solely to love. It is as if she receives with both hands, carefully, the love the Son brings to her (which is the love of Father, Son and Spirit), so that nothing shall be lost and she can look after it and hand it on to others.

With this immense love Mary lives as a human

being among other human beings, but as someone who is privileged to live with the Son and has a preeminent share in his whole destiny. She keeps in the background so that the whole light falls on him and the eyes of believers rest on him. And if, occasionally, she has to say some word or show herself, she only does it to direct attention to him.

This love is very great; not merely does it transcend the Mother's earthly life and, just as she accompanied her Son's life, accompany the life of Christians, continually creating joy, Christian surprise and deeper dedication; it is so great that it also transcends the death of every person. The Mother was there when the Son died, but she is always present when anyone is dying; she makes no distinction in her love between the Son of Man and his brethren. She has expanded her accompanying of her Son to universal proportions; she accompanies us all in a helping, ministering way. She puts at our disposal everything she has received. Her love's everlasting fruitfulness is felt particularly where a dying person is afraid he will no longer encounter love; where, at the end of his life, he realizes that he has loved too little, believed and hoped too little. Then she takes loving steps, encouraging new love, new hope and faith to sprout. The form this takes is, "Let it be to me according to your word", for the dying man can do nothing but let things happen, unquestioningly and in total surrender.

So the meaning of death is unveiled through the

unveiling of the life of the Mother and the Son; accompanying us at our death, she accompanies us in a life that stretches beyond death into eternal life. The Mother was assumed bodily into heaven. But this assumption was so complete and perfect and glorious that it was too much for her alone. Its grace is complementary to the grace of her pre-redemption, and she can dispense it to anyone who encounters her in confession (where too the absolution is greater than the sin, and the absolved person must hand on what he has received) or in any sacrament, especially in the sacrament of the dying, for on the basis of her Son's death she knows what dying means, and because of her immediate elevation to heaven she knows what the heavenly encounter means. She wishes to communicate this grace of the heavenly encounter so that the dying person need not stare solely at death and judgment but can look to the grace granted to the Mother and the mediation of all graces. The Son gives a new meaning to the life of every believer, but together with his Mother he fulfills every death by creating new room for love and hope in the midst of death. The new beginning sets out from this point. The loss of earth opens up the gaining of heaven.

In the beginning, out of love, God created the human being as man and woman. But man and woman have sinned and deserved death. In view

of this offense to God, death had to be an un-
yielding penalty. But God's mercy and love are
greater than his will to punish. Death remains as a
warning, but it is also the decisive means of becoming worthy of seeing God's face, through
accepting the purification he chooses. As a means
of giving death the character of mercy, God the
Father chose his love for the Son, but, since their
reciprocal loves continually vie with each other,
he also chose the Son's love for him and his work.
And he has allowed the new Eve, together with
the new Adam, to imbue death with the quality of
mercy. Furthermore, he has given death the character of penance, by making it, together with
purgatory, into a purification. Nor was this
enough: he permitted the Mother to be assumed
bodily in heaven so that the Father should have a
counter-image to the creation: the first couple had
betrayed him; the last couple loved him above
everything. Looking at this couple, the dying man
is assured of the superior power of love over
death. Not only has the circle come around again
to paradise; it has been surpassed, for death is
swallowed up in eternal life.

20-21 LBLetz = cult/a fear + death —

48 & peace & complete
surrender

48-9 & meaning of my life
(+ my death)

53 death as "a word
from god"

62 our death = "& final concentration
+ our surrender to god"

62-3 & form + ovd is
from god, not us —

72 J on+   84 Living "come follow me"
cross   ★ — demands too great —
                     faithfulness

— 94 for & saint, d co +
"open door"

107 & contemplative
vocation

112 & result + &
sacrament for dying,

113-14 'falling into god —
+ in + + love

★123 Mary is always
present when
anyone is dying